GCSE Modern World History

EXAM REVISION NOTES

Richard Staton
John Wright

Philip Allan Updates, part of the Hodder Education Group, an Hachette Livre UK company, Market Place, Deddington, Oxfordshire OX15 0SE

Orders
Bookpoint Ltd, 130 Milton Park, Abingdon, Oxfordshire, OX14 4SB
tel: 01235 827720
fax: 01235 400454
e-mail: uk.orders@bookpoint.co.uk
Lines are open 9.00 a.m.–5.00 p.m., Monday to Saturday, with a 24-hour message answering service. You can also order through the Philip Allan Updates website: www.philipallan.co.uk

© Philip Allan Updates 2002

ISBN 978-0-86003-442-1

Photographs are reproduced by permission of Topham Picturepoint and Peter Newark's Pictures.

Design by Juha Sorsa
Cover illustration by Neil Fozzard
Printed in Malaysia

Philip Allan Updates' policy is to use papers that are natural, renewable and recyclable products and made from wood grown in sustainable forests. The logging and manufacturing processes are expected to conform to the environmental regulations of the country of origin.

Contents

Revision and the path to exam success

How to use this book

Revision is vital for success in your GCSE examinations. No one can remember what they studied over a two-year course without a reminder. To be effective, revision must be planned. This book provides a carefully organised course and this is how to use it.

Step 1 Check the contents list and select those topics you need to revise. Make a note of the topics you need to learn for Paper 1 and for Paper 2.

Step 2 These revision notes give you the facts you need to know. Read the notes carefully and summarise each topic, reducing it to 20–30 bullet points on one side of paper (see *Revision rules* box on page vi).

Step 3 If you have time, further summarise these bullet points onto small index cards. This will help you when you are short of time just before the examination date, since having a small number of cards from which to revise is a lot less daunting.

Step 4 Read the *Exam watch* boxes. They will give you an idea about the likely focus of examination questions.

What do the examiners want?

Command words

All examination questions include command or action words. These will tell you what the examiner wants you to do. Here are some of the most common ones:

Describe... Give detailed facts or information about what happened, not why it happened.

Explain or give reasons for... Show understanding by giving reasons why something took place.

According to the source... or **What does the source tell us?** Describe in your own words what information is contained in the source. This does not require you to add to the answer by using extra knowledge.

Use the source and your own knowledge... The important point here is to LINK the information contained in the source with other detailed knowledge from outside it. You must add to what the source contains.

Compare the sources — why do they say different things? *Explain* the differences rather than simply saying how they are different.

Do you agree that...? Provide a balanced answer giving both sides of the argument. For example: 'Germany was to blame for the start of the First World War. Do you agree? Explain your answer.' Here you must explain why Germany was to blame *and then include other reasons* for the start of the First World War.

(a) Causes, consequences and change

GCSE examination papers will ask you to:

- *describe* events in the past, e.g. how things have changed
- explain *why* events happened
- explain the results or consequences of a particular event

What will help you improve the quality of your answers?

Step 1 Look at what the question wants and always stick to the point.

↓

Step 2 Explain the part played by each reason as the cause of an event or as the result of the event.

↓

Step 3 Remember that each event would have many causes or results.

↓

Step 4 If you think that one reason or result was more important than any of the others, explain why that reason was more important and the others less so.

↓

Step 5 Support your ideas with accurate details.

↓

Step 6 Don't forget a conclusion to sum up your answer.

↓

Step 7 LINK different reasons or results together by showing:
- how one cause might have led to another
- how some causes depended on others happening first
- how the entire event could not have happened without one vital reason being present

(b) Understanding sources

All GCSE History papers ask you to study historical sources. These include:

- visual sources — photographs, paintings, drawings, cartoons
- written sources — letters, history books, newspapers, diaries, memoirs, official reports, speeches, statistics
- 'modern' media — TV documentaries, drama, film, radio

Ask yourself these questions:

Step 1 Have you described what the source tells you?

↓

Step 2 Have you explained if the author of the source can be trusted to produce an accurate/reliable piece of evidence?

↓

Step 3 Have you included some factual information to test if the source is reliable or unreliable?

↓

Step 4 (to be used if the question asks if a source is useful) Have you explained the gaps in the information contained in the source — that its usefulness depends not only on what is being asked about the source but also on what the source misses out?

Questions you might be asked include:
- Are the sources... reliable, useful, accurate, biased?
- 'What do the sources suggest about...?'
- 'Why are the sources different?'
- 'Is there sufficient information in the sources to prove...?'
- 'What problems might a historian face when using the sources?'
- 'Is the source a fair interpretation?'

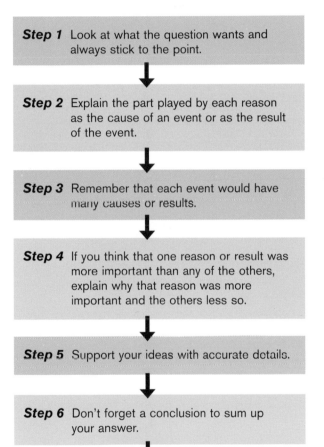

Key points to remember

Do you know

The exam board setting your paper?

↓

How many papers you will be taking?

↓

The date, time and place of each paper?

↓

How long each paper will be?

↓

What the subject of each paper will be?

↓

What the paper will look like? Do you write your answer on the paper or in a separate booklet?

↓

How many questions you should answer?

↓

Whether there is a choice of questions?

↓

Whether any part of the paper is compulsory?

↓

If you don't know the answer to any of these questions as the exam approaches — ask your teacher!

Revision rules

Start early.

↓

Plan your time by making a timetable.

↓

Be realistic — don't try to do too much each night.

↓

Find somewhere quiet to work.

↓

Revise thoroughly — reading is not enough.

↓

Summarise your notes, making headings for each topic and bullet points.

↓

Ask someone to test you.

↓

Try to answer some questions from old papers. Your teacher will help you.

↓

If there is anything you don't understand — ask your teacher.

Be prepared

The night before the exam

Complete your final revision.

↓

Check the time and place of your examination.

↓

Get your equipment ready (pens, pencils etc.)

↓

Go to bed early and set the alarm clock!

On the examination day

Don't rush.

↓

Double check the time and place of your exam and your equipment.

↓

Arrive early.

↓

Keep calm — breathe deeply.

↓

Be positive.

Examination tips

Keep calm and concentrate.

↓

Read the paper through before you start to write.

↓

If you have a choice, decide which questions you are going to answer.

↓

Make sure you can do all parts of the questions you choose, including the final sections.

↓

Complete all the questions.

↓

Don't spend too long on one question at the expense of the others.

↓

Stick to the point and answer questions fully.

↓

Use all your time.

↓

Check your answers.

↓

Do your best.

Britain and
WWI
1914–18

Britain's reaction to the First World War

Why was war so popular in 1914?

The declaration of war on Germany was met with great enthusiasm. There was little under-standing of the bitter struggle to come. There were a number of reasons why the British people were eager to engage in conflict with Germany:

- Rivalry between Britain and Germany had been growing for some time.
- Britain felt challenged by the growth of the German navy and so had built a new class of battleship — the Dreadnought. But Britain did not need a bigger navy. The sense of rivalry increased.
- Stories in the press had built up a fear and dislike of Germany.
- Britain controlled a huge empire and there was a feeling that no one should be allowed to challenge its prime position in the world.
- When war broke out in August, there was a bank holiday in Britain — the 'holiday' feeling across the country developed almost into hysteria. Men flocked to join the army.
- The notion that the war would be 'over by Christmas' was very strong. It would be exciting — but brief. It was important to defend 'little Belgium' against the 'barbaric Hun'.
- There was high unemployment in parts of Britain and taking the 'King's shilling' (private soldiers were paid a shilling a day) meant a job, with regular meals.
- The new Secretary of State for War, Lord Kitchener, was a national hero and his appointment guaranteed support for the war.

The Kitchener poster — a prominent feature of the recruitment campaign

Recruitment, 1914–18

Huge numbers of men flocked to join the army in August and September 1914. It was a 'lark' — but a patriotic one. Economic uncertainties caused by the war led to some 500,000 redundancies. Many of these men joined the army.

Men also joined up because their friends did — the 'herd instinct'. Lots of volunteer units became famous, such as the Accrington Pals, the Barnsley Pals, the Tyneside-Scottish etc. By the end of December 1915, 2.5 million men had joined the army without any legal compulsion.

1914	1.18 million
1915	1.28 million
1916	1.19 million
1917	0.82 million
1918	0.49 million

Numbers of men recruited into the British army

Methods of recruitment

Initially, the moral pressure from women-folk, friends and acquaintances, together with posters and recruiting songs, were very effective. However, by early 1915 the numbers joining up began to slow down. Unemployment had fallen and, as news came through of increasing numbers being killed, there was a diminishing attraction in going to the Front.

Thus, there had to be **changes** in the methods of recruitment:

♦ In August 1915 all single men were placed on a National Register and were pressured to 'attest' to undertake to serve in the army, if and when called upon to do so. Skilled workers were given exemptions. This was the Derby scheme.

♦ Only half of the single men on the National Register attested. So in January 1916 the Military Service Act was introduced. All single men were liable to conscription. This was the first time there had been conscription in Britain.

♦ A second Military Service Act was passed in May, which included all males between the ages of 18 and 41.

When conscription was finally introduced, it marked the lowering of the remaining barriers of prejudice to the full-scale employment of women.

Exam watch

Questions tend to focus on change from voluntarism to compulsion. Revise the causes of these changes.

Conscientious objectors

Once conscription had been introduced for all males following the second Military Service Act in May 1916, it was difficult to avoid joining the army. If a man wished to be excused service, he could do so on four grounds:

(1) being physically unfit
(2) having a job which was essential to the war effort — a 'reserved occupation'
(3) having responsibility for a family, such that his dependants would suffer if he was conscripted
(4) having reasons of conscience for not wanting to fight

RALLY ROUND THE FLAG

WE MUST HAVE MORE MEN

Tribunals

To avoid conscription, a man had to appear before a military tribunal. Tribunals were made up of military personnel and civilians. They could reach one of four decisions:

a **Absolute exemption** — the individual was found to be unconditionally exempt from military service.

b **Conditional exemption** — the man had to become involved in work of national importance.

c **Exemption from combatant duties** — the man must join the armed forces, but would not be required to fight. These men usually worked in ambulance units.

d **Rejection of the request** — the man had to join the army.

Conscription produced two kinds of conscientious objectors: non-combatants, who joined the army; and the 'Absolutists', who refused to perform any military service at all. It also brought a new word into the English language — 'conchie' — a term used to shame, belittle and embarrass those who refused to fight on grounds of conscience.

What happened to the Absolutists?

There were about 1,500 Absolutists. They were considered to be traitors, cowards, and even criminals, by the vast majority of people in Britain. Many factory owners would not employ the 'conchies'. Prison camps were set up and the Absolutists were sentenced to 'hard labour' — breaking rocks or sewing mailbags. The camps were closed in 1919.

73 Absolutists died as a result of the harsh treatment they received in prison and 31 went insane as a result of their experiences.

Men who had fought in the army and were 19 or 20 were allowed to vote in the 1918 general election — but the 'conchies' were disenfranchised.

Why were 'conchies' important?

They helped to safeguard an individual's right to freedom of choice and expression.

The high profile of conscientious objectors served to make people recognise their own obligations.

In a perverse way, they were good for morale.

Thousands of conscientious objectors did heroic work that did not involve fighting. Many Quakers served as ambulance-men in the front lines and won medals for their bravery there.

J. Brooman, *The Great War*, 1985

 Exam watch

Questions may focus on the descriptive side — 'What were COs…?', 'How were COs treated…?' (think of the main points) — and 'Explain…'.

The role of the British government

The government wanted to ensure that it had control of all aspects of the war effort. As the war developed, more restrictions were introduced.

🔑 Key points

- As soon as war broke out, the government passed the Defence of the Realm Act, giving it extensive powers. There were restrictions on hoarding food and profiteering; trade union rights were limited; and the government was able to control rents and prices. It could also seize land and horses, if necessary.
- In 1916 British Summer Time was introduced for the first time and the opening hours of public houses were limited. Alcoholic drinks were watered down — and buying rounds of drinks was banned!
- The government thought it important to stoke the public's hatred of the enemy and did so by publishing propaganda posters, which publicised so-called German atrocities. In 1915 the first films to encourage support for the war effort were made, and in 1916 the film of the Battle of the Somme was shown in cinemas all over Britain. It was watched by more than 20 million people.

In 1915 a crisis arose due to a shortage of shells for the artillery in France. This gave the government an opportunity to take control of the munitions industry. Lloyd George became Minister of Munitions in 1915; he was responsible for ensuring that the munitions industry provided the armed forces with all necessary weaponry. By 1918, the ministry had a staff of 65,000 and employed over 3 million workers in about 20,000 factories.

In 1915 the government drew up a National Register, to ensure that all adults played their part in the conflict. The role of the government continued to grow when, in 1916, it passed two Military Service acts, which introduced conscription.

Lloyd George became Prime Minister in 1916 and he increased government control of industry. His policies became known as 'War Socialism' and ministries were set up for food production and shipping. A government minister took charge of the railways and the production of coal was overseen by a government controller.

To combat food shortages, a Food Controller was appointed and farmers were encouraged to grow more. Wheat and potato production increased significantly.

In order to pay for the war, the government raised taxes. By the end of the war, the number of income taxpayers had increased from 1.5 million to 7.75 million. This was one change that would not be reversed after the war.

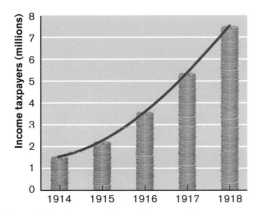

Growth in the number of income taxpayers

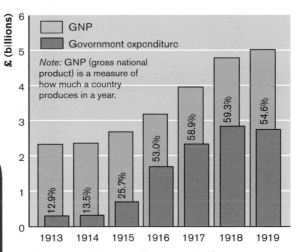

Government expenditure as % of gross national product

Lloyd George set up a Ministry of Reconstruction in 1917. This was a clear indication that the government recognised its obligations to the people. It was a sign that the war had brought about some positive changes.

 Exam watch

Questions tend to focus on how the role of government changed. Ensure you know about DORA, munitions, control of industry, aspects of everyday life — 'War Socialism'.

 Don't forget

Although the government took control of much of Britain's industry during the war, it was quick to 'de-control' in the years 1918–22. It was only after the Second World War that large parts of industry were 'nationalised' and came under the ownership of the government.

Rationing

🔑 Key points

- Shortages of food only became a serious issue for the government at the end of 1916. In 1917 there were shortages of sugar, potatoes, margarine and coal — and shoppers had to queue for these items.
- Before the war, Britain had imported about 60% of its food; and when the German U-boats proved successful in sinking merchant ships in 1916 and 1917, concern in the government grew.

Sugar	100%
Butter	65%
Cheese	80%
Bacon	65%
Wheat	80%
Fruit	40%

Percentages of food imported in 1913

Lord Devonport was appointed Food Controller in 1917. However, he was incompetent and was replaced by Lord Rhondda, who proposed a system of voluntary rationing, with people allocating themselves 'meatless' days and tea-shops

putting their own limits on the types of food to be sold.

As the price of bread and potatoes rose, the government stepped in and introduced subsidies. (At this time it was not unusual for an agricultural labourer to rely almost entirely on bread for his main diet, eating between 6 and 7 kg per week.)

Food production was taken under government control and rationing was introduced in January 1918. Not only were

Ration card

some food stocks low, there was also hoarding of goods. At first rationing applied only to meat, but in July sugar, butter, margarine and cooking fat were added.

Food sold in restaurants was also controlled and customers had to hand over coupons with their order. Rationing had the perverse effect of increasing food consumption, because most people bought their full rations, even if they did not actually need them or want them.

The weekly bread allowance for men was 7 pounds (3.2 kg) and for women 4 pounds (1.8 kg). Children under six were given half the meat ration and adolescent males and men working on heavy jobs were allowed a food supplement. However, the allowance was not always taken up, because poor people could not afford to do so.

Meat	24 ounces	(680 gms)
Butter or margarine	4 ounces	(113 gms)
Sugar	8 ounces	(227 gms)

Rations per person per week in 1918

Rationing continued after the end of the war. A double meat ration was allocated for Christmas 1918, but the rationing of meat did not end until late in 1919. Butter rationing stopped early in 1920 and the rationing of sugar was removed later that year.

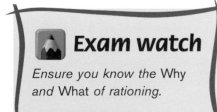

Exam watch

Ensure you know the Why *and* What *of rationing.*

Don't forget

Rationing was yet another aspect of government control with which people were unfamiliar. Never before had the government exercised such influence and control over the details of their lives. Everyone returned to 'normality' with a considerable sense of relief. However, in January 1940, during the Second World War, the government introduced restrictions on a much greater scale (see page 33).

The impact of the war on people in Britain

In 1914 the people of Britain could not remember a time when war had touched them directly. Young men went off to fight, and some did not return. But throughout the prosperous Victorian period, wars were events which took place usually in far-away lands. However, this war soon developed into one which brought the front line to the ordinary citizen.

The first modern war which had a 'Home Front' included the following:

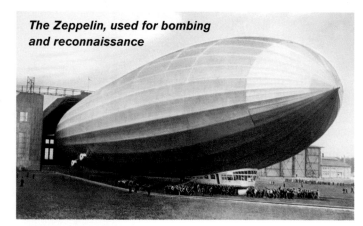
The Zeppelin, used for bombing and reconnaissance

- In December 1914 German battlecruisers bombarded Yarmouth, Scarborough, Whitby and Hartlepool along the east coast. Scarborough was shelled for about 45 minutes and 19 people were killed and 80 wounded.
- From January 1915 German airships known as Zeppelins began to make bombing raids on British cities. The first raids were on Yarmouth and King's Lynn in East Anglia, close to the North Sea coast. Subsequent attacks were as widespread as Merseyside, Sheffield, Burton-on-Trent and London. The raids on London in June 1917 killed 162 people and injured 432. Altogether there were 51 Zeppelin raids.
- From the end of 1915, the Germans began air-raids using Gotha bombers. By the end of the war there had been 57 such raids.
- Total civilian casualties in Britain during the First World War were 5,611, of which 1,570 were killed (1,413 in air attacks).

The health of the nation

The effects of the war on the diet of the British people were not all adverse. They led to:

Reduced alcohol and sugar consumption

Increased consumption of bread and potatoes

Bigger meals and higher calorie intake — men away at the front, and women especially, ate much better than many of them had been used to

Industrial canteens being set up, more school meals provided and the extension of health insurance

 Exam watch

Questions can often focus on how civilians were brought into contact with danger — bombers/Zeppelins — as well as rationing etc. Give examples of places where civilians were attacked.

The impact of the war on women

🔑 Key points

- Before the war, the most common employment for a woman was as a domestic servant. However, women were also employed in what were seen to be suitable occupations.
- When war broke out in August 1914, thousands of women were sacked from jobs in dressmaking, millinery and jewellery making. They needed work — and they wanted to help.
- Suffragettes ceased all militant action in order to support the war effort.
- Initially, there was much trade union opposition and the employment of women had not increased significantly before the summer of 1915. In July 1915, a 'Right to Work' march was organised by a leading suffragette, Christabel Pankhurst.

- The shell shortage crisis in 1915 began to change the situation. Women were taken on to work in munitions factories. The government did a deal with the trade unions, known as the Treasury Agreements. The unions agreed to accept female labour in place of men 'for the duration of the war'.
- The introduction of conscription in 1916 led to an increase in the number of women employed in all sectors of the economy.
- Many women were paid good wages, especially in munitions factories, but in most cases they were paid far lower rates than men.
- Improved wages did permit greater independence for some women.
- Women became more 'visible' in the world of work. They were seen to be doing important jobs.
- The armed forces also employed women, but the jobs were mainly of a clerical and domestic nature.
- Women were much in demand for the 'caring' side of employment and became nurses in the First Aid Nursing Yeomanry, and drivers and clerks in Voluntary Aid Detachments.

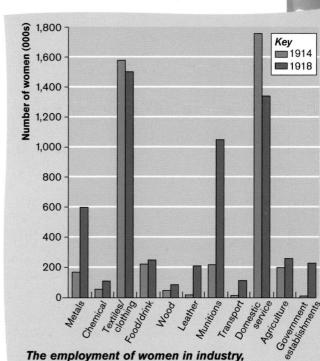

The employment of women in industry, 1914 and 1918

The legacy of war

At the end of the war, there was great optimism in Britain and a firm belief that the sacrifice could not, and should not, have been in vain. Lloyd George spoke of building a 'land fit for heroes' and there was an expectation that all the returning soldiers would have a job and a decent place to live. Lloyd George planned to build a million new homes. In fact, only 200,000 were completed, but the government had taken on a new responsibility for its citizens — a dramatic change from the pre-war years.

By 1939 unemployment benefit was available for twelve months, although only the man in the family qualified. The same was true for sickness benefit and medical treatment.

However, the postwar optimism gradually disappeared. This was because:

- Dislocation caused by the war, and the sudden cessation of armaments production, led to economic recession and widespread unemployment. Many returning soldiers became embittered by their inability to find work.
- The cost of the war had been massive and the government did not have the financial resources to fulfil all its promises.
- The Depression of the 1930s made these problems worse.

What was the outcome of women's contribution to the war effort?

On the negative side...

- By 1918 some newspapers had become critical and negative about the role of women in the war.
- Most women involved in wartime employment lost their jobs after the armistice was signed.
- Many women found employment again — but often in domestic service.

On the positive side...

- Many women over 30 were granted the vote in 1918. They had to be householders, or married to a householder. Working-class women who had contributed to the war were still disenfranchised.
- However, all women over 21 were granted the vote in 1928 — at last gaining equality with men in the franchise.
- The first woman to take her seat in Parliament (Nancy Astor) was elected in 1919.
- The first female cabinet minister (Margaret Bondfield) was appointed to the Labour government of 1924.

By 1939, as war again threatened Europe, it was clear that much remained to be done for the 'welfare' of the British people. Many felt that the struggle and sacrifice of the Great War had resulted in a waste of lives.

 Exam watch

Questions will tend to look at change — it is therefore important to give some background. Remember it is not until 1915 that changes for women occur. Questions also ask if there was lasting change — look at issues after 1918.

Peace and conflict 1919–39

The Treaty of Versailles

Did the terms of the treaty satisfy the peacemakers?

On 11 November 1918 the guns fell silent and the First World War came to an end. When the peacemakers arrived at the Palace of Versailles just outside Paris, it was clear that the Allies had different ideas about how Germany should be treated. Should Germany be crippled, or just punished? Was it possible to deal with Germany in a just way, so that the peace would last? The 'Big Three' made the crucial decisions.

President Woodrow Wilson — the United States

Woodrow Wilson believed in harmony and peace. He had high ideals — Germany would certainly have to be punished, but not so harshly as to seek vengeance in the future. The world, he thought, would be a safer place if nations co-operated with each other. A fair peace would make war less likely.

The United States, having joined the war in April 1917, suffered fewer casualties and less damage than any other nation. Wilson's ideas for peace were based on a speech made in January 1918. The ideas in this speech were called the Fourteen Points and included:

- no secret agreement between states
- free access to the seas for all nations
- countries to guarantee armament reduction
- colonies to be given a say in their own future
- Belgium to be restored
- France to recover its land, including Alsace-Lorraine
- self-determination for the people of Austria-Hungary
- an independent Poland to be set up with access to the sea

Prime Minister Clemenceau — France

Clemenceau saw an opportunity both to punish Germany and to cripple it permanently, so that French security would be guaranteed. France had lost 1,358,000 men and the 10% of its land that had been occupied was devastated. The coalmines of the Saar region were flooded as the German army pulled back in 1918.

Clemenceau also sought vengeance for France's defeat by Prussia in 1871. He was not interested in whether Germany could afford to pay — the ruin of Germany would make it incapable of attacking France in the future. France wanted the return of Alsace-Lorraine, the Saar coalfield as compensation, and an independent Rhineland state to shield it from Germany. France's war debt was huge and Clemenceau favoured a demand for very substantial reparations (payments) from Germany.

Prime Minister Lloyd George — Britain

Britain had been scarred by 4 years of war. Over 761,000 men had been lost and the war had cost Britain £8,000 million. Nearly every family had suffered loss. The British propaganda machine had whipped up hatred against Germany; the 1918 General Election was dominated by slogans such as 'Hang the Kaiser' and 'Make Germany pay'.

However, Lloyd George favoured a moderate peace. He knew that a vindictive treaty might lead to German bitterness and demands for revenge. Even so, he supported the proposal that Germany should be stripped of its colonies and navy, which were seen as threats to Britain.

The terms — what Germany lost

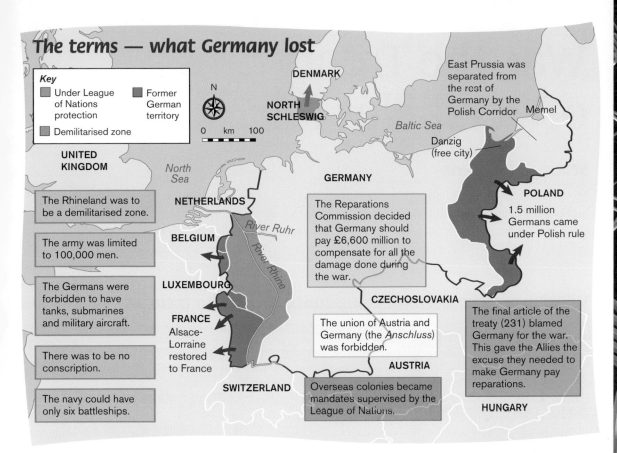

Key
- Under League of Nations protection
- Demilitarised zone
- Former German territory

0 km 100

N

DENMARK

NORTH SCHLESWIG

NORTH SEA

North Sea

Baltic Sea

East Prussia was separated from the rest of Germany by the Polish Corridor

Memel

Danzig (free city)

UNITED KINGDOM

NETHERLANDS

GERMANY

River Ruhr

River Rhine

BELGIUM

LUXEMBOURG

POLAND

1.5 million Germans came under Polish rule

FRANCE
Alsace-Lorraine restored to France

CZECHOSLOVAKIA

AUSTRIA

SWITZERLAND

HUNGARY

The Rhineland was to be a demilitarised zone.

The army was limited to 100,000 men.

The Germans were forbidden to have tanks, submarines and military aircraft.

There was to be no conscription.

The navy could have only six battleships.

The Reparations Commission decided that Germany should pay £6,600 million to compensate for all the damage done during the war.

The union of Austria and Germany (the *Anschluss*) was forbidden.

Overseas colonies became mandates supervised by the League of Nations.

The final article of the treaty (231) blamed Germany for the war. This gave the Allies the excuse they needed to make Germany pay reparations.

Who was satisfied with the settlement?

Clemenceau
He wanted a harsher peace. So did the French people, who now voted him out of power.

The French thought that Germany should have been punished, with the Rhineland and the Saar region removed from Germany permanently.

Clemenceau thought that reparations should be as large as possible, and that the USA had been too generous. After the war the French felt let down by America, which withdrew from involvement in European affairs in the 1920s and turned its back on defending France.

Wilson
He said the settlement was too harsh on Germany. The United States Congress rejected it. This also meant that the USA would not become a member of the League of Nations, founded in 1920.

Lloyd George
Although hailed as a hero, he was also disappointed with the treaty. He feared that Germany would be left a bitter and resentful country, looking for the first opportunity to tear up the treaty. In addition, he felt that Wilson's desire to impose self-determination on the postwar world looked like an attack on the British Empire.

Was the Treaty of Versailles fair?

Setting the scene

When the Germans read about the Treaty of Versailles, they were bitter and angry that they had been treated so harshly. German newspapers spoke of 'revenge for the shame of 1919'. The German people were shocked in defeat: newspapers had not prepared them for the collapse of 1918. Were the Germans correct in their verdict — that the Treaty of Versailles was a disgrace?

What were the German complaints about the treaty?

Germany was going to be ruined by such harsh terms.

It would take many years to pay all the reparations.

Germany had lost too much land (13%) and far too many people (12%).

Germany had been forced to sign the treaty. It was a 'diktat' or dictated peace, with no negotiation by Germany. Wilson's Fourteen Points had stated that it would be openly discussed.

The Fourteen Points said all nations were to disarm, but Germany had been made defenceless — left with a small army and tiny navy. However, Britain and France had not disarmed, leaving Germany vulnerable.

Germany was obliged to sign the treaty prior to the decision about the scale of reparations.

Germans had not been allowed self-determination, as promised by Wilson in the Fourteen Points. Many Germans lived outside Germany — in Austria, Czechoslovakia and Poland, for example.

Overseas lands (colonies) had been taken from Germany and given as mandates to Britain and France (despite the principle of self-determination).

The concept of war guilt had forced Germany to accept the blame for the war.

The Fourteen Points were offered as ideas for peace. What did the Germans do in the Spring of 1918? They attacked the Allies in a last attempt to win the war. This was a rejection of the Fourteen Points.

The German war machine had inflicted great damage and Germany had to pay for it.

German disarmament would make the world a safer place.

The Allies' reply to German complaints

Germany was not ruined. In the 1920s it became prosperous again. By 1925 steel production was greater than Britain's.

Germany had no right to complain, having treated Russia so badly at the Treaty of Brest-Litovsk in 1918. Russia lost half its industry and one-third of its people. It showed that if Germany had won, it would have been harsh on the losers.

Whatever we think now about the treaty, the Germans were bitter at the time. On the other hand, there were some hopeful signs that things might improve.

Bitterness
- France feared Germany and invaded the Ruhr in 1923 when reparations were not paid.
- Reparations kept Germany weak, and high taxes and inflation made life difficult.
- There was an army of occupation.
- The Maginot line was built by France as a defence against Germany.
- Germany's neighbours did not disarm after the war.

Hope
- Germany joined the League of Nations in 1926.
- Germany signed the Locarno Pact of 1925 (see page 43).
- The Dawes Plan of 1924 gave Germany loans to help recovery.
- Germany signed the Kellogg–Briand Pact in 1928 — and was no longer an outcast.

 Exam watch

Focus on explaining the aims of the Big Three and how far each was dissatisfied with the final Treaty of Versailles. Was it fair? What were the main reasons for the German hatred of it? Support your answers by using the terms of the treaty. As you revise from the following pages, consider the impact of the treaty on the 1920s and 1930s. What problems did it cause in the long term?

Germany's defeated allies: Austria, Hungary, Turkey

🔑 Key points

◆ While the future of Germany was being decided at the Palace of Versailles, other treaties were being signed around Paris in 1919 and 1920:
  ● Austria — Treaty of St Germain, 1919
  ● Bulgaria — Treaty of Neuilly, 1919 (by which it had to pay reparations and accept a much reduced army)
  ● Hungary — Treaty of Trianon, 1920
  ● Turkey — Treaty of Sèvres, 1920
◆ President Wilson of the USA wanted the peoples of Central and Eastern Europe to have self-determination.

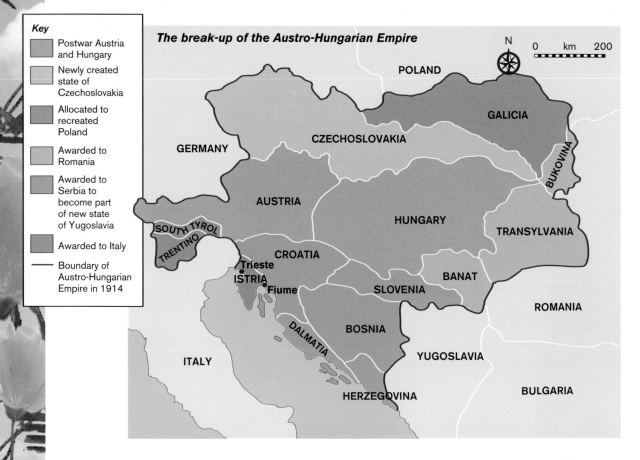

The break-up of the Austro-Hungarian Empire

Key
- Postwar Austria and Hungary
- Newly created state of Czechoslovakia
- Allocated to recreated Poland
- Awarded to Romania
- Awarded to Serbia to become part of new state of Yugoslavia
- Awarded to Italy
- Boundary of Austro-Hungarian Empire in 1914

Austria agreed to...

◆ accept the formation of the new states of Czechoslovakia, Yugoslavia and Poland
◆ give Italy Trentino, Trieste, the South Tyrol and Istria
◆ give Eastern Galicia to Poland
◆ have a smaller army of 30,000 men
◆ pay reparations to the Allies
◆ a clause in the Treaty forbidding *Anschluss* with Germany

Austria

Austria was bitter because it...

◆ lost two-thirds of its land
◆ lost three-quarters of its people
◆ lost rich farming land and industry
◆ was forced to apply for loans

Hungary agreed to...

◆ give land to Czechoslovakia, Austria and the new Yugoslavia
◆ give Transylvania to Romania
◆ pay reparations to the Allies
◆ reduce its army to 35,000

Hungary

Hungary was bitter because it...

◆ lost two-thirds of its land
◆ lost half its roads and railways
◆ lost valuable timber and iron ore deposits

Problems caused by the peacemakers

The shading shows groups of people who were left behind in a foreign country once the map of Europe was redrawn. There were 3 million German-speaking people in Czechoslovakia, and 30% of the people living in Poland were not Polish.

Some of the newly-created countries were vulnerable, too small and faced economic problems.

Italy was disappointed because it expected to receive more land than it did as a reward for joining the war on the side of the Allies.

Poles

Czechs

Ruthenians

Slovaks

Germans

Germans

Magyars of Hungary

Rumanians

Tyrol

Transylvania

N

Southern Slavs

Italians

Minorities left in 'foreign' states after the break-up of Austria-Hungary

0   km   200

Key

/// Minorities

Turkey

Turkey was the only country to oppose the peace terms successfully. The leader of the Turks, Mustafa Kemal, led a campaign to recover the land lost at the Treaty of Sèvres. A new treaty was signed at Lausanne in 1923.

Turkey

◆ regained the land lost to Greece
◆ did not pay reparations
◆ but did not regain its colonies, which had been given as mandates to Britain and France

The League of Nations

What were the aims of the League of Nations?

Founded in 1920, the League of Nations was based on the last of Wilson's Fourteen Points. The **Covenant**, or rules, formed the first 26 articles of the Treaty of Versailles. The League of Nations aimed to safeguard peace through **collective security** — all members agreeing to protect each other from attack. Members promised not to attack other states. To make the world a safer place, the League was to try and persuade countries to sign a Disarmament Treaty. It aimed to change agreements or treaties between countries if they endangered world peace. Disputes had to be submitted for discussion and aggressive nations could be punished by applying economic sanctions (banning trade) or military sanctions (the use of force).

How was the League organised?

Special Commissions

These were set up to deal with world problems — disarmament, health (dealing with disease and the problem of drugs), mandates, refugees and minorities. Much was done to reduce the incidence of diseases such as leprosy and malaria, to stop slavery, and to help re-settle refugees.

The Secretariat

The Secretariat was like a civil service, carrying out the day-to-day administration of the League.

The council met three times a year or when there was an emergency.

It made the important decisions, if action was needed.

In 1920 the Council had four permanent members: Britain, France, Italy and Japan. The USA should have been one of these, but it never actually joined the League.

At first, there were four non-permanent members, which sat on the Council for 3 years at a time. This was later increased to nine members.

Council

Assembly

The International Labour Organisation (ILO)

This was very successful; it took measures against unemployment, and campaigned for an 8-hour day, better wages and conditions, sickness and injury benefits, as well as old-age pensions.

This was the parliament of the League, because representatives of all its members met once a year.

The Assembly could decide to take action, accept new members into the League, or vote on which countries should be non-permanent members of the Council.

Could the League have worked and kept the peace?

Yes Powerful countries were weary of war, and the memory of the trenches and killing fields of Belgium and France meant that there was a strong desire for peace. The League established firm rules — and if determined action was taken against those who broke them, then peace stood a chance. With the USA taking the lead as the world's most powerful nation, the League might have worked.

No The League had significant weaknesses.

◆ The USA rejected the League and refused to join.
◆ The League was associated with the hated Treaty of Versailles and was seen as a 'club' for the winners. Britain and France were accused of selfishly using the League for their own ends.
◆ The shadow of the war began to be replaced by resentment about the harshness of the peace treaties. This weakened some nations' motives to strive for peace.
◆ The League's rules were not properly thought through. Permanent members of the Council each had a veto, and unanimous action was difficult to achieve. All decisions made in the Assembly had to be unanimous too. In addition, if a country decided to attack another, it was supposed to give 3 months' notice! This was clearly unlikely to happen.
◆ These rules were difficult to change.
◆ If a country broke the rules, would firm action be taken? If a country was willing to tear up the map of Europe, could anything be done to force it to back down?
◆ Collective security could not work when some countries were missing from the League, as the chart below shows.

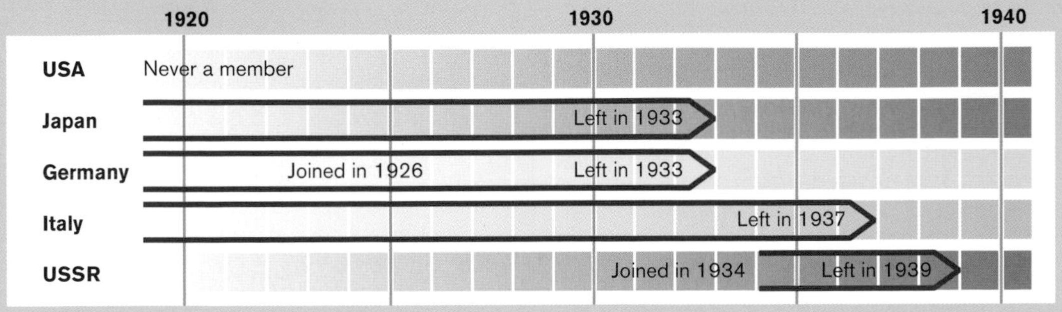

BRITAIN: was it committed to the League?

GERMANY: the priority was to alter the terms of the Treaty of Versailles

FRANCE: the priority was to keep Germany weak

ITALY: a permanent member, which still broke the rules in 1923 and 1935

Map labels: NORWAY, FINLAND, SWEDEN, ESTONIA, USSR, LATVIA, LITHUANIA, North Sea, UNITED KINGDOM, NETHERLANDS, BELGIUM, GERMANY, POLAND, CZECHOSLOVAKIA, Atlantic Ocean, FRANCE, AUSTRIA, HUNGARY, ROMANIA, SWITZERLAND, ITALY, YUGOSLAVIA, BULGARIA, PORTUGAL, SPAIN, ALBANIA, GREECE

	1920	1930	1940
USA	Never a member		
Japan		Left in 1933	
Germany	Joined in 1926	Left in 1933	
Italy		Left in 1937	
USSR		Joined in 1934	Left in 1939

The League in the 1920s: hopes of peace?

Hopes were high that the League of Nations could settle disputes in the 1920s. It was believed that collective security would protect the smaller nations. The special agencies were also busy at work. Overall, did the League succeed in the 1920s?

Disputes settled

Upper Silesia, 1921

This was a rich iron and steel producing area coveted by both Germany and Poland. The League organised a plebiscite (referendum) and it was successfully divided up. The industrial areas went to Germany, the rural areas to Poland.

The Aaland Islands, 1921

Sweden and Finland were threatening to go to war over these disputed islands. The League became involved and decided that the islands should go to Finland. The matter was settled when Sweden agreed to this.

War between Bulgaria and Greece, 1925

Greece invaded Bulgaria when some Greek soldiers were killed on the border. The League intervened, ordering Greece to stop the invasion and withdraw its soldiers. Greece was also told to pay compensation to Bulgaria and the whole matter was settled when Greece obeyed the League's instructions.

In 1926 Germany joined the League of Nations as a full member.

Disputes which the League failed to settle

Vilna, 1920

Vilna was the capital of Lithuania, a newly-created state. In 1920 a Polish general seized it. The League failed to act in this crucial test. France and Britain should have condemned Poland and forced its troops to leave. But they were keen to keep on good terms with Poland, which acted as a buffer between Germany and Communist Russia. In the end Polish aggression was allowed to stand.

Turkey and Greece, 1920

Turkey took matters into its own hands, when the Paris peacemakers decided what it should lose under the Treaty of Sèvres. Turkey attacked Greece and recovered some of the land it had lost. The League failed to stop the aggression.

Corfu, 1923

An Italian general was shot and killed while surveying the border between Greece and Albania. The Italian dictator, Mussolini, demanded compensation and bombed the Greek island of Corfu. What would the League do? It said Italy had been in the wrong to bomb Corfu, but that Greece should pay compensation. The League proposed to keep the money until those guilty of the murder were arrested.

Mussolini was furious. He refused to accept the League's decision and the delay. He asked the Conference of Ambassadors to force Greece to pay the 50 million lire due immediately. When the money was paid, it looked as if the League had been by-passed and an aggressor had got his own way.

Did the League make any progress on disarmament?

Little was done to bring about universal disarmament. Germany had been forced to disarm by the Treaty of Versailles.

The only achievement was the signing of an agreement at the Washington Conference of 1921 by Britain, France, the USA and Japan. It forbade the building of battleships for 10 years and then limited the numbers each navy could have.

Further talks on disarmament came to nothing when Germany walked out of the League in 1933.

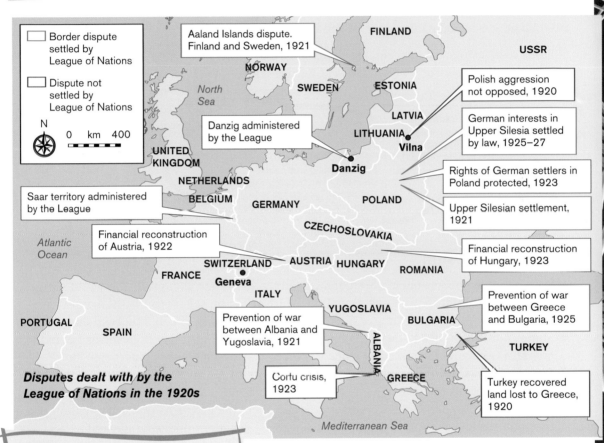

Key:
- Border dispute settled by League of Nations
- Dispute not settled by League of Nations

N

0 km 400

FINLAND

USSR

NORWAY

SWEDEN

ESTONIA

LATVIA

LITHUANIA

Vilna

North Sea

Aaland Islands dispute. Finland and Sweden, 1921

Polish aggression not opposed, 1920

German interests in Upper Silesia settled by law, 1925–27

Danzig administered by the League

Rights of German settlers in Poland protected, 1923

Danzig

UNITED KINGDOM

NETHERLANDS

BELGIUM

GERMANY

POLAND

Upper Silesian settlement, 1921

Saar territory administered by the League

CZECHOSLOVAKIA

Financial reconstruction of Austria, 1922

Atlantic Ocean

SWITZERLAND

AUSTRIA

HUNGARY

ROMANIA

Financial reconstruction of Hungary, 1923

FRANCE

Geneva

ITALY

YUGOSLAVIA

BULGARIA

Prevention of war between Greece and Bulgaria, 1925

PORTUGAL

SPAIN

Prevention of war between Albania and Yugoslavia, 1921

ALBANIA

TURKEY

Corfu crisis, 1923

GREECE

Turkey recovered land lost to Greece, 1920

Disputes dealt with by the League of Nations in the 1920s

Mediterranean Sea

Exam watch

Focus on explaining the weaknesses of the League from the start. Did these mean that the League would inevitably fail? Were the successes of the 1920s significant? Was the period generally one of hope — or of concern for the future?

Were there signs of a more peaceful future in the 1920s?

As the 1920s drew to a close, there was a sense of more settled times. Although the League had had its failures, and little had been done to achieve international disarmament, some useful agreements had been signed, namely:

- The Locarno Pact (see page 43)
- The Kellogg–Briand Pact (see page 43)
- The Dawes and Young Plans (see page 42)

The League in the 1930s: failure and conflict

The Wall Street Crash

What was the Wall Street Crash? Why did it make it more difficult to keep the peace? In October 1929 there was panic selling of shares on Wall Street in New York. In one month, $40 billion was wiped off the value of US shares.

Millions of investors lost their money; companies and banks failed; and the American government recalled all the loans which had kept Europe going in the 1920s. This led to a world depression.

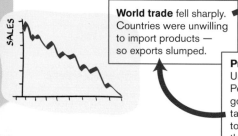

World trade fell sharply. Countries were unwilling to import products — so exports slumped.

Investment fell and businesses found it harder to find buyers for their products. Prices collapsed.

Production fell and so did wages. Unemployment began to rise. People had less money to buy goods. Some countries placed tariffs (taxes) on imported goods to protect their own industries, thus restricting trade even further.

World depression

◆ With 12 million people unemployed, the United States market collapsed. The world's largest economy had stuttered to a halt. Countries which relied on selling to the US market were quickly caught up in the slump, e.g. Brazil (coffee), Argentina (meat) and Australia (wool).

◆ Some countries turned to dictatorships and extreme solutions to get themselves out of the crisis. In Germany the Nazi Party came to power, claiming it was the 'last hope' for Germany. In Italy Mussolini decided to develop an overseas empire, to take people's minds off their problems at home.

◆ Britain, France and the USA were so concerned about the problems of the Depression that they put less effort into international peacekeeping, sanctions and disarmament.

◆ Meanwhile, in 1931 Japan invaded Manchuria.

The League fails: 1 Manchuria

Japan		Manchuria	
Half of its factories were idle. Exports had collapsed and Japan desperately needed new markets and raw materials.	The Japanese army seemed to be in control of foreign policy. Its answer was to expand overseas.	Manchuria was the ideal target for Japanese expansion. It had coal, iron ore, timber and markets for Japanese goods.	In September 1931 an explosion took place at Mukden, near to the Japanese-owned South Manchurian railway. Blaming China for this, Japanese forces occupied the province of Manchuria.

The League had failed. Why?

Japan was too far away. Britain and France were not willing to go to war on the other side of the world. The USA and the USSR were the only powerful countries which might have taken effective action, but neither belonged to the League. A strong, militaristic country had proved that force could succeed.

- China asked the League for help.
- A Commission of Enquiry was sent to investigate. It took a year to produce its report, which said that Japan had been the aggressor and should withdraw.
- Japan, in the meantime, set up a satellite state, renaming Manchuria the Manchukuo.
- Japan left the League in 1933 and invaded Jehol, another province of China.

The League fails: 2 Disarmament

In February 1932, the Disarmament Conference met. Those attending knew that little had been done about the threats from chemical weapons, aerial bombing and the increasing size and power of tanks. And what was to be done about Germany, which claimed that it should be treated more fairly and as an 'equal'? Germany alone had been forced to disarm after Versailles. No one else had done so. When France finally refused to allow Germany to rearm up to the level of other nations, Hitler walked out of the conference (October 1933).

 Exam watch

Focus on why the League failed to keep the peace in the 1930s, including how far the Depression undermined its work.

The League fails: 3 Abyssinia

1 Mussolini was keen to establish an overseas empire. An attempt by Italy to invade Abyssinia (now Ethiopia) in 1896 had failed. Following a border dispute at Wal Wal in 1934, Mussolini had the excuse he wanted. In October 1935 Italy invaded Abyssinia.

2 Britain and France both wanted to avoid a quarrel with Italy. These three countries had just signed the **Stresa Front**, a defensive agreement aimed against Germany and Hitler. However, when the Emperor of Abyssinia, Haile Selassie, asked the League for help, something had to be done. **Collective security** had to be demonstrated.

3 Sanctions were imposed on Italy. Fatally, however, the League put off a decision about whether to stop oil supplies to Italy. In addition, the Suez Canal was not closed to Italian shipping. The Italian war machine rolled on.

4 To make matters worse, news leaked out that the British and French foreign ministers, Hoare and Laval, had hatched a plan to give Mussolini two-thirds of Abyssinia if the invasion was stopped. The League and its two most powerful nations, Britain and France, appeared weak, by giving in to aggression.

5 By May 1936 Italy had conquered the whole of Abyssinia and the League had failed its final big test. Italy prepared to leave the League, which it did in 1937.

In the years up to the Second World War, 1938-39, the League played no significant role in trying to keep the peace.

Causes of the Second World War
The background, 1919–38

The long shadow of the First World War

The bitterness of the war, and German resentment about the Treaty of Versailles, cast a long shadow over the 1920s and 1930s. France had aimed to ruin Germany after the First World War, but continued to be worried about the threat of attack.

French fear of Germany after 1919

On the one hand, France had:
- regained Alsace-Lorraine
- made Germany pay massive reparations
- gained control of the Saar for 15 years
- ensured the demilitarisation of the Rhineland on the border with Germany

On the other hand, France was not satisfied with the Treaty and would have preferred a much harsher one (see page 14).

So France took more action to ensure its safety.
- Treaties were signed with east European states — Poland, Czechoslovakia, Hungary, Yugoslavia and Romania.
- The Maginot line was built.
- The Stresa Front was signed in 1935 between France, Britain and Italy, with the aim of placing a defensive net around Germany.

The Wall Street Crash

The crash on the US stock market led to the Depression. These catastrophes also brought Hitler to power in 1933 (see page 46).

Hitler's foreign policy aims

Hitler wanted to:
- destroy the Treaty of Versailles
- create a greater Germany to include all Germans living outside the country

- carry out the *Anschluss* (union with Austria)
- gain *Lebensraum* (living space) for the German people with land taken at the expense of the Poles and Russians
- rearm
- destroy the hated French and Communist Russia

1934 Germany failed to achieve *Anschluss*. Nazis murdered the Chancellor of Austria, Dollfuss, and Hitler appeared to be getting ready to invade. However, he was stopped by Mussolini, who moved part of the Italian army to the border with Austria as a warning.

1935 People of the Saar voted by 9 to 1 in a plebiscite to rejoin Germany.

1935 Germany openly announced rearmament. An extra 850,000 men were to be conscripted into the army. Plans were made to build 95 warships and 8,250 warplanes by 1939.

1933 Germany left the Disarmament Conference and the League of Nations.

1931 1932 1933 1934 1935 1936 1937 1938 1939

1937 The Anti-Comintern Pact was signed between Germany and Japan to fight Communism. The world's three most militaristic powers were now linked by agreements.

1936 Hitler signed the Rome–Berlin Axis agreement with Mussolini.

1935 The Anglo–German Naval Agreement was signed in 1935. It was agreed that Germany should build ships up to 35% of the number in the British navy. This broke the terms of the Treaty of Versailles.

1936 The Rhineland demilitarised zone was reoccupied by the German army.

1937 Hitler sent help to General Franco in the Spanish Civil War. The Germans used this as a training ground for their tank crews and Luftwaffe pilots.

 FOCUS ON *Reoccupation of the Rhineland, 1936*

According to the Treaty of Versailles and the Locarno Pact, the Rhineland was to remain a demilitarised zone. However, with the world's attention focused on Abyssinia — the League of Nations looking on helplessly — Hitler seized his chance.

In March 1936 he ordered his generals to reoccupy the Rhineland. It was a bluff. The German army was not yet strong enough to resist an attack from France. Hitler gambled that the French would do nothing. He was right. Britain felt that Germany had been unjustly treated at Versailles and had some sympathy with the reoccupation. France would not lift a finger without British support. The German army remained in the Rhineland unopposed.

Causes of the Second World War
Appeasement

Both the public and politicians in Britain and France feared the horror of war. Not only did they have vivid memories of the trench warfare of 1914–18, but the destruction of Guernica in 1937 by German planes in the Spanish Civil War highlighted people's fear of aerial bombing. The British government had estimated that there might be over a million casualties from bombing raids in any future war.

Was Hitler the real enemy? Some politicians thought not. They considered that the greater threat came from Stalin, the leader of the USSR. If so, Germany would be a useful barrier against the spread of Communism from the East.

Why did Britain and France believe that appeasement was the best policy after 1935?

In Britain the Treaty of Versailles was regarded as harsh and unjust. There was sympathy for the view that Germany should regain some lost land and should not be left defenceless, as its neighbours had failed to disarm.

If, as Neville Chamberlain (the British Prime Minister) thought, Hitler was a reasonable man, then if German demands could be satisfied, war would be avoided and peace secured.

British and French armed forces were unprepared for a major war. Appeasement would at least allow a breathing space so that military preparations could be made.

Anschluss 1938: the union of Germany and Austria

Why?
Hitler was an Austrian by birth. The Treaty of Versailles had forbidden the *Anschluss* to take place. However, if Hitler's aim of self-determination for all Germans was to be achieved, then a good place to start was Austria — whose people, by race, are German.

What happened?
Hitler sent for Schuschnigg, the Austrian Chancellor, and demanded that the ban on the Austrian Nazis should be lifted and that a Nazi should take an important post in the Austrian government.

Schuschnigg did not give in. He planned to organise a plebiscite, hoping for a vote which might enable him to oppose Hitler's plans. However, Hitler began to make new threats. He would use the Austrian Nazis to wage civil war, making 'another Spain of Austria'. Fearing bombings and political murders, the Austrian government gave in. In March 1938 German troops were invited into Austria. *Anschluss* was achieved.

The Czechoslovakian crisis, 1938–39

Phase 1 Munich and the Sudetenland 1938

Appeasement had already been seen in action. Where?

◆ the Anglo–German Naval Agreement of 1935
◆ attitudes in Britain towards the remilitarisation of the Rhineland, which had taken place unopposed
◆ the *Anschluss*, which had taken place unopposed apart from some small-scale protests
◆ German rearmament, which had continued with neither Britain nor France taking action to stop it

The Sudetenland Crisis

In 1938 there was increased tension about the Sudetenland, which was part of Czechoslovakia. Three million Germans lived there and Hitler was encouraging the Sudeten Germans to demand that they should join the Third Reich. Hitler complained that these Germans were being denied their civil rights by the Czech government.

Key
▨ Sudetenland
■ Anti-tank fortifications
⌐ Armaments plant

Something had to be done. France had an alliance with the Czechs, who had a powerful army to protect their country. Chamberlain's attitude was to appease Hitler. He thought that the British would not be willing to fight about a 'quarrel in a far-away country'. To avoid war, he flew to see Hitler three times during 1938. The final meeting took place at Munich in September.

Munich

It was here that an agreement was signed between Britain, France, Italy and Germany. The Czech leaders were left out of the talks — the news that the Sudetenland was to be handed over to Germany was broken to them by the British and French. Hitler had won a great victory without a shot being fired. As the Sudetenland contained important anti-tank defences, the loss of the area left Czechoslovakia open to attack. Hitler was delighted.

Chamberlain Grasping a peace agreement signed by Hitler, he claimed to have secured 'peace in our time'.

The Czechs They felt abandoned by their allies and vulnerable to attack.

What lessons were drawn from Munich?

Hitler Once again he had succeeded in winning land without a shot being fired. He was convinced that Britain and France would not stand up to him — encouraging him to demand more land.

Stalin He lost all faith that Britain and France would stand up to Hitler. Stalin now felt that an alliance with Britain or France might be worthless.

GCSE Modern World History

Causes of the Second World War

The lead-up to war, 1938–39

Phase 2 The destruction of the rest of Czechoslovakia

◆ Hitler continued to make threats against what was left of Czechoslovakia. Slovaks and Germans inside the country wanted more rights.

◆ In March 1939 President Hacha of Czechoslovakia gave in to Hitler, who wanted more 'protection' for the Germans who lived there. Hitler was threatening to bomb Prague. German troops were 'invited' to occupy the country. Czechoslovakia disappeared from the map. Once again nothing was done to stop Hitler and even Chamberlain realised that he could not be trusted. Appeasement was dead.

Key

▢ Gained under Munich Agreement (September 1938)

▢ Occupied by Germany (March 1939)

▢ Independent, but under German protection (March 1939)

The carve-up of Czechoslovakia

The final act — war against Poland

Poland was next. The Polish Corridor and Danzig, both seized under the Treaty of Versailles, were the targets.

Britain and France promised to help Poland with military aid, if it was attacked. They also tried to gain the support of Stalin, but without success. Stalin was already convinced that Britain and France were weak and would not stand up to Hitler. The world was shocked when, in August 1939, the Nazi–Soviet Pact was signed. This was a non-aggression pact between Hitler and Stalin. They agreed not to attack each other and to divide Poland between them.

On 1 September Germany attacked Poland. On 3 September Britain and France declared war on Germany. They had stood by their alliance with Poland and decided that Hitler must be stopped by force. The Second World War had begun.

 Exam watch

Focus on explaining the impact on the following in causing the war:

◆ *the terms of the Treaty of Versailles*
◆ *Hitler's aims and strategies*
◆ *the League of Nations*
◆ *the Depression*
◆ *the USA's isolationism*
◆ *rearmament*
◆ *appeasement*
◆ *the USSR (Nazi–Soviet Pact)*

What was the relative importance of these long- and short-term factors? Why did appeasement not prevent war? Why did Britain and France eventually go to war in 1939?

Britain and WWII
1939–45

Britain's reaction to the Second World War

When war broke out in 1939, some preparations had already been made for the 'Home Front'. Gas masks had been produced for everyone and air-raid shelters had been constructed.

Evacuation

The government decided to evacuate children and other vulnerable people from areas that were likely to be bombed. The bombing of Guernica in the Spanish Civil War and of Shanghai during the Japanese invasion of China suggested that there would be large-scale civilian casualties.

On the move: the dislocation of war

- Britain was divided into three regions: evacuation, neutral and reception areas. The whole transport system was taken over for the purpose of evacuation.
- Evacuation had begun in June 1939 and by early September some 3.5 million people had been evacuated.
- Children were moved in school groups with their teachers. They were allowed to take one suitcase and had labels around their necks in case they got lost. In the reception areas, host families were allowed to choose the evacuees they wanted.
- Evacuation led to a complete mixing of social classes. Children from middle-class families were sent to live with working-class families and vice versa.
- Many people were horrified at the state of health of evacuees who came from city centres.
- Many children were not accustomed to an inside toilet, running water, carpets, baths; they often did not change their clothes regularly and were infested with lice or were suffering from skin diseases like scabies. Some were not used to eating a balanced diet.
- The government had to give money to local authorities to provide clothes for the poorest children.

Area	
London	Under 50%
Lancashire towns/cities	66%
Stoke and the Black Country	25%
Sheffield	15%
Rotherham	8%

Numbers of children evacuated during the war

Rationing

Rationing began in January 1940 and was not finally removed until 1953. At first, only some foods were rationed; but clothing, soap and furniture were all added later.

- ◆ Rationing was brought in first of all to ensure that there were adequate supplies of food. Britain produced about half the food it needed; the rest was imported.

- ◆ A committee was set up to decide how much nutrition people in different jobs required. Workers in heavy industry got more, as did pregnant women.

- ◆ It was hoped that rationing would ensure a healthy and balanced diet for all Britons.

- ◆ Everyone was then issued with a ration book and had to register with a butcher and a grocer. They were supplied with enough food for their customers.

- ◆ Special supplements were made available for young children; orange juice and cod liver oil became common and lasted long after the war. The government also produced artificial meats such as SPAM and MOR.

More than 50% of working people began to keep allotments. These were largely in response to the 'Dig for Victory' campaign, which encouraged people to grow as much of their own food as possible. By 1943 there were 1,400,000 allotments in Britain.

Rationing did improve the nation's health. It forced people to eat less of the foods that were bad for them and more of the foods which were healthy. Consumption of potatoes rose by 40%, vegetables and milk by 30%.

The role of government

Rationing had a profound effect on the formation of government policy. Previously it was not believed possible to make major changes to the nation's health. Many politicians thought this was not the concern of government. Together with the plight of the poor, which was revealed by evacuation, rationing helped to change these views.

Rationed foods	Non-rationed foods
Sweets, meat, butter, jam, cheese, fats	Vegetables, bread, potatoes, fish, milk*

(*Milk was in fact rationed, but the ration was 3 pints a week — an increase for most people.)

Petrol	September 1939
Butter, bacon and sugar	January 1940
Meat	March 1940
Tea and margarine	July 1940
Sale of silk stockings banned	December 1940
Cosmetics (except lipstick)	February 1941
Clothes	June 1941
Points system for rationing introduced	November 1941

Rationed goods and dates of rationing

The civilian war

The Blitz

The Blitz was the period of heavy bombing of British cities by the German air force, the **Luftwaffe**, which took place chiefly during September, October and November 1940. When the Luftwaffe lost the Battle of Britain for fighter domination of the skies, attention was turned to bombing raids.

The government had issued over 2 million Anderson shelters to civilians to erect in their back gardens. In addition, many communal shelters were provided underground. A 'blackout' had also been enforced; all lights had to be hidden at night. Nonetheless, the winter of 1940–41 was very difficult, as bombing destroyed homes, lives and families. Every major town and city in the British Isles was attacked.

Effects of the Blitz

The worst affected city was London, where 13,000 people were killed in 1940. In the rest of Britain about 10,000 people were killed.

Bombing came in several forms. The most common bombs were incendiaries, small bombs which burnt fiercely. The Germans also used high-explosive bombs; but the most dangerous were mines, which drifted down on parachutes and exploded later.

Coventry was hit by a very heavy raid in November 1940, which destroyed the centre of the city and killed about 500 people. Other cities, such as Belfast, Hull, Portsmouth and Plymouth, also suffered heavy raids.

The Blitz was intended to break the morale of the British people, as well as to disrupt industrial production.

At first bombing was concentrated on central London, particularly the docks. German planes followed the line of the Thames and then dropped their bombs on the East End. Damage was severe, not only to buildings but also to morale.

From early in 1941, however, attacks on Britain became less serious. The last major raid was on Belfast in April, which killed more than a thousand people. Hitler was turning his attention to the invasion of the Soviet Union.

Response to the Blitz

◆ To tackle the effects of bombing, the British government set up a series of Auxiliary Services, of which the ARP was one. Air Raid Precaution wardens were appointed for every street. They had the job of checking houses and they had to be told how many people were sleeping in each house each night.

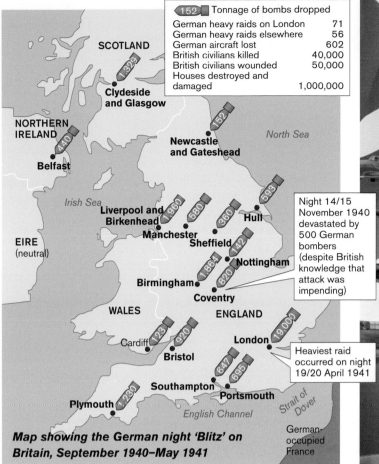

Tonnage of bombs dropped

German heavy raids on London	71
German heavy raids elsewhere	56
German aircraft lost	602
British civilians killed	40,000
British civilians wounded	50,000
Houses destroyed and damaged	1,000,000

Night 14/15 November 1940 devastated by 500 German bombers (despite British knowledge that attack was impending)

Heaviest raid occurred on night 19/20 April 1941

Map showing the German night 'Blitz' on Britain, September 1940–May 1941

◆ The Observer Corps watched for planes on high buildings, counting and identifying them for the RAF controllers after they had been picked up on radar.
◆ The government created the Ministry of Information, which produced many films advising people about regulations. The main emphasis in every film was on keeping calm and maintaining discipline.
◆ At first, London Underground stations were not used as shelters. However, the early attacks were so severe and so damaging to morale, that this decision was reversed. One of the first stations to be opened was Bethnal Green in the East End.

The Home Guard

The Local Defence Volunteer Force was set up in July 1940, but the name was changed almost immediately to the Home Guard. It became known as 'Dad's Army' and was mostly made up of older men, often former soldiers. At first, units had no uniforms and few weapons, but they eventually became more organised.

The Home Guard's main role was to take over home duties from the regular army. The part-time soldiers patrolled beaches, stood sentry duty at nights and weekends and even rounded up German pilots after they were shot down.

Home Guard battalions were also trained to carry on a guerrilla war following a German invasion, and secret hide-outs were constructed.

V1 and V2 rockets

- In 1944–45 Britain was attacked from the air once again. About 20,000 people were killed in rocket attacks from France and the Netherlands.
- The first attacks came from pilot-less rocket planes called V1s (known as 'doodlebugs'). These could be launched from railway trucks, which were moved from place to place. Each rocket carried about 1 tonne of explosive, and when it ran out of fuel it fell to the ground and exploded.
- V1s flew at about 350 miles per hour and could be shot down, but the resulting explosion could be very dangerous.
- Some pilots attempted to bring the V1s down over open country by flying alongside them and tipping them over with the end of their wing. This upset the balance of the V1, which was controlled by a gyroscope.

The role of women

During the war the number of women working in Britain doubled to more than 7 million. Over 500,000 women were in the armed services.

Conscription for unmarried women was introduced in 1942. This was later extended to married women without children.

Conscription was introduced so that women could fill non-combatant roles in the armed forces.

A number of convenience foods were invented to give women more time to work.

For the first time, women were recruited on a large scale for skilled jobs.

In 1945 there were campaigns to persuade women to give up their jobs, just as there had been in 1918; but this time, despite pressure, many women stayed on.

The Butler Education Act of 1944 gave all girls secondary education for the first time.

- The most successful method of dealing with the V1, however, was to move most of the anti-aircraft guns around London down to the south coast, and shoot down the rockets as they came over.
- The successor to the V1 was the V2, which was a much more serious threat. They were real rockets, which were fired from sites in Holland. They could not be shot down and no defence against them was successfully developed.

Exam watch

Focus on the impact of the war on the civilians and how the government tried to overcome problems. Look for key differences experienced by civilians in the two world wars. Be prepared to compare the role of women in 1914–18 and 1939–45.

Propaganda and the media

The Ministry of Information controlled all the media in Britain and ensured that no information was published which might damage the war effort. News and propaganda was put out in print, on the radio and on film.

- Posters covering every aspect of life were issued by the ministry.
- People came to rely on the radio. By the end of the war, there were almost 11 million radio licences in Britain.
- Most people visited the cinema at least once a week.
- Many films were pure propaganda, but they helped to cement the feeling of common purpose.

Beginnings of the welfare state

The Beveridge Report

In 1941 the government asked Sir William Beveridge to head a Royal Commission to consider all existing social insurance schemes. Beveridge discovered that it was not fruitful to look at some areas of insurance and not others; all aspects of social life were inter-linked. So he widened his brief. The Beveridge Report was published in 1942.

Beveridge recommended that the people of Britain should be protected from 'five giants': **squalor**, **ignorance**, **want**, **idleness** and **disease**. The Report explained how this could be done. Beveridge said that the government should take responsibility for the welfare of the people of Britain, 'from the cradle to the grave'.

The Report was very timely because:

- The Rowntree Report of 1936 had shown that poverty still existed in Britain and about 10% of the population suffered real hardship.

- The suffering of the British people during the war convinced many politicians that action must be taken.

- The evidence of **evacuation** showed what the lives of some people in Britain were like. Many evacuees were in very poor health. In 1941 a report was published by the Women's Institute revealing that evacuees suffered from infestations of lice and diseases caused by malnutrition.

- **Rationing** showed that government intervention could be effective. In addition, the government provided dietary supplements for the first time, such as orange juice and cod liver oil. These had a major impact on the health of children.

- The Beveridge Report became a bestseller. The government said that it was going to set up a **welfare state** as soon as the war ended. The first part of the Beveridge Report was put into place in 1944 when an Education Act was passed.

The Butler Education Act, 1944

The Act provided for a Ministry of Education to replace the Board of Education. This immediately showed that the government was giving education greater priority. It also implemented the following changes:

- All fees for state schools were abolished.
- The school leaving age was to be raised to fifteen.

- For the first time, all children would attend secondary school. At the age of eleven they would take a test, the 'eleven plus', to decide what form of secondary education was appropriate for them.
- There were to be three types of state schools — grammar, secondary modern and technical. All three types of schools were to enjoy equal status and have equal resources.

The 1944 Act marked an important change in educational policy in Britain. For the first time the government accepted that all children had a right to secondary education free of charge.

The welfare state

After the general election of 1945, the new Labour government began to implement the Beveridge Report. How was the welfare state to be organised?

- National Insurance contributions became compulsory. For one payment a week, everyone received a whole range of benefits: **unemployment benefit**, the **old age pension**, **sickness benefit**, a widow's pension etc.
- **Family allowances** were paid to mothers to help support their children.
- Benefits were paid to everybody and there was no limit to the length of time that they could be claimed.

Making a claim for family allowances, June 1948

A newly built Chelsea council flat, 1948

- The **National Health Service** was set up in 1948 and provided medical services free of charge. The service included free visits to a doctor and free prescriptions, free hospital treatment, and free dental and optical treatment.
- The National Assistance Board gave grants to people who fell below the poverty line.
- The Housing Acts of 1946 and 1948 led to more than 800,000 council houses being built, in addition to 150,000 prefabricated houses. The effects of bombing meant that a major house-building programme was essential.

Germany
1918–45

The Weimar Republic

 Key points *A bad start for postwar Germany*

- By October 1918 Germans faced the shock of unexpected defeat. Their great army was unable to carry on fighting.
- The British naval blockade had brought starvation to a Germany which faced economic ruin. Socialists encouraged workers to strike. German sailors at the Kiel naval base mutinied when officers ordered them to attack the British.
- The Kaiser (Wilhelm II) fled to Holland. How would Germany be ruled?
- In the 'November Revolution', Fredrich Ebert, leader of the Social Democratic Party, said elections would take place and that Germany would become a republic.
- Ebert signed an armistice, bringing the fighting to an end. As a result, he and other politicians became known as the 'November criminals', because they had 'stabbed the German army in the back'.
- Germany was in chaos; strikes, violence and bloodshed on the streets of Berlin forced the government to move to the small town of Weimar.
- After elections, Ebert became President of the Weimar Republic.

The Weimar Constitution

- Germans were used to being ruled by a kaiser, so they found it difficult to accept rule by a parliament (the Reichstag).
- All men and women over 20 had the vote.
- Voting was by proportional representation — parties won the same proportion of seats in the Reichstag as the number of votes cast. This meant that many small parties existed and weak coalition governments had to be formed. Members of coalitions often argued between themselves and so governments were short lived.
- The president had emergency powers and *could* rule on his own without the Reichstag — rather like a dictator.

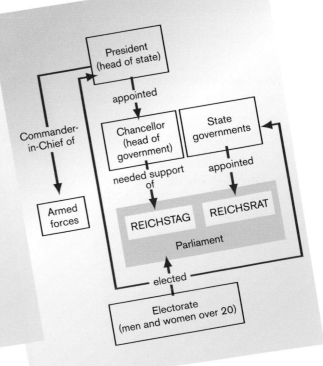

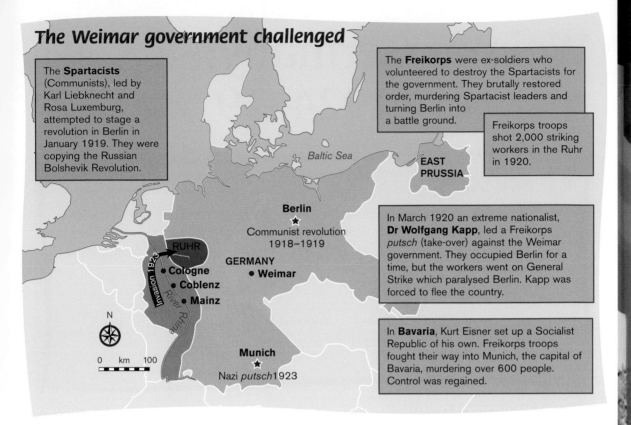

The Weimar government challenged

The **Spartacists** (Communists), led by Karl Liebknecht and Rosa Luxemburg, attempted to stage a revolution in Berlin in January 1919. They were copying the Russian Bolshevik Revolution.

The **Freikorps** were ex-soldiers who volunteered to destroy the Spartacists for the government. They brutally restored order, murdering Spartacist leaders and turning Berlin into a battle ground.

Freikorps troops shot 2,000 striking workers in the Ruhr in 1920.

Baltic Sea

EAST PRUSSIA

Berlin
Communist revolution 1918–1919

GERMANY
• **Weimar**

RUHR
• **Cologne**
• **Coblenz**
• **Mainz**

Invasion 1923

River Rhine

N

0   km   100

Munich
Nazi *putsch* 1923

In March 1920 an extreme nationalist, **Dr Wolfgang Kapp**, led a Freikorps *putsch* (take-over) against the Weimar government. They occupied Berlin for a time, but the workers went on General Strike which paralysed Berlin. Kapp was forced to flee the country.

In **Bavaria**, Kurt Eisner set up a Socialist Republic of his own. Freikorps troops fought their way into Munich, the capital of Bavaria, murdering over 600 people. Control was regained.

Economic problems

The Reparations Commission finally decided in 1921 that Germany would pay £6,600 million as compensation for the damage done to the Allies. By 1922 it was clear that Germany could not pay. As a result, French and Belgian troops occupied the Ruhr, Germany's main industrial area. If Germany would not pay, then the Allies would seize the coal and steel for themselves.

The Weimar government ordered passive resistance. Germans were told not to obey French and Belgian instructions and were to go on strike. Violence erupted. Germans were arrested, deported and in all 132 people were killed.

Without any industrial wealth, and in order to pay the workers, the Germans printed money. This caused **hyper-inflation**. Money had no value. Many Germans were ruined — pensioners and middle-class professional people lost their savings. Workers' wages could not rise quickly enough to keep pace with the loss in value of the mark. Once again, Weimar was blamed.

	1918	0.63 marks
	1922	163 marks
January	1923	250 marks
July	1923	3,465 marks
September	1923	1,512,000 marks
November	1923	201,000,000,000 marks

The cost of one loaf of bread, 1918–23

Hitler, the little-known leader of the Nazi Party, decided the time was right for a revolution. In November 1923 he announced a march on Berlin from a Munich beer hall (see page 45). Although his putsch failed and he was imprisoned, support for his action showed the deep unpopularity of the Weimar Republic.

Weimar Germany: recovery, 1924–29

Key points

- In August 1923 Gustav Stresemann took over as Chancellor, then as Foreign Minister.
- His immediate problem was to deal with inflation.
- He ended passive resistance in the Ruhr and persuaded the French and Belgians to withdraw from German soil.
- The worthless banknotes were burned and a new currency, the *Rentenmark*, was issued.
- Stresemann aimed to help German industry recover with loans from the United States, and to sign agreements with its old enemies so they might start to trust Germany again.

Economic recovery

The Dawes Plan, 1924

USA
Charles Dawes was an American banker. He arranged for reparations to be paid in instalments, starting at £50 million, in line with Germany's ability to pay. US loans then poured into Germany.

Britain and France
Both countries had borrowed heavily from the USA during the war. As Germany recovered, reparation payments were resumed, and Britain and France were able to repay loans to the USA.

Germany
Loans were used to rebuild factories, install machinery and increase production levels. New houses and public buildings were constructed and Germany got back to work. Unemployment did fall, but only slowly.

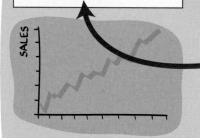

The Young Plan, 1929

Germany was further helped by another American plan, which brought reparations down to £2,000 million — to be paid over 59 years.

Germany: still the enemy?

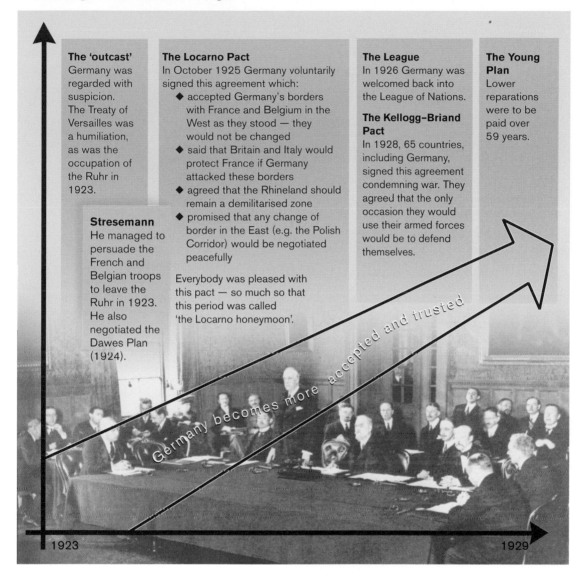

The 'outcast'
Germany was regarded with suspicion. The Treaty of Versailles was a humiliation, as was the occupation of the Ruhr in 1923.

The Locarno Pact
In October 1925 Germany voluntarily signed this agreement which:
- ◆ accepted Germany's borders with France and Belgium in the West as they stood — they would not be changed
- ◆ said that Britain and Italy would protect France if Germany attacked these borders
- ◆ agreed that the Rhineland should remain a demilitarised zone
- ◆ promised that any change of border in the East (e.g. the Polish Corridor) would be negotiated peacefully

Everybody was pleased with this pact — so much so that this period was called 'the Locarno honeymoon'.

The League
In 1926 Germany was welcomed back into the League of Nations.

The Kellogg–Briand Pact
In 1928, 65 countries, including Germany, signed this agreement condemning war. They agreed that the only occasion they would use their armed forces would be to defend themselves.

The Young Plan
Lower reparations were to be paid over 59 years.

Stresemann
He managed to persuade the French and Belgian troops to leave the Ruhr in 1923. He also negotiated the Dawes Plan (1924).

Germany becomes more accepted and trusted

1923   1929

A false dawn?

By 1929, Germany seemed to have recovered. But there had been little progress towards disarmament — and was Germany relying too much on loans from the United States?

In October 1929, the Wall Street Crash would begin the Depression — and ruin Germany's recovery.

 Exam watch

Questions on the Weimar Republic up to 1929 tend to focus on whether it was doomed from the start and how far Germany had recovered by 1929. The First World War and the Treaty of Versailles both had an important impact on Weimar and you should be prepared to analyse their short- and long-term effects.

The growth of the Nazi Party

Hitler: the early years

1889 Born in Austria, the son of a customs official. At school Hitler was a lazy pupil, who achieved very little.

1907 He failed to gain acceptance to the Academy of Fine Arts in Vienna. When he was turned down as a trainee artist he fell into poverty, living in hostels and drifting from job to job.

1914–18 He was in Munich when the First World War broke out. He enthusiastically joined the German army, serving on the Western Front throughout the war.

1918 Hitler was shocked by defeat, but he remained a soldier, spying on left-wing political extremists.

1919 He joined the German Workers' Party and soon became one of its most important members.

1920 The German Workers' Party was renamed the National Socialist German Workers' (Nazi) Party and published a 25-point programme.

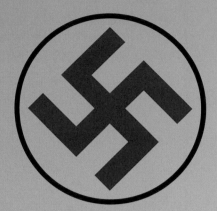

The Nazi symbol was a swastika, an ancient religious sign, with a prominent red colour to appeal to socialists

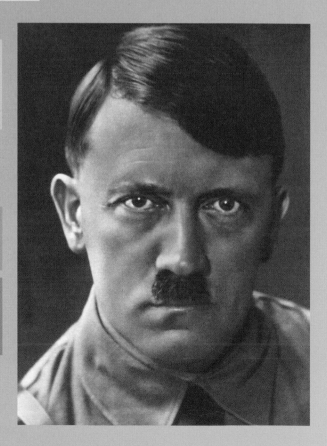

The Nazis' 25-point programme

There was something for everyone in the Nazi's 25-point programme — nationalists, socialists, the middle classes, the old and racists. Among other things it demanded:

1 The union of Germans to form a greater Germany.

2 Abolition of the Peace Treaties.

3 Land to feed the German people.

4 That only those of German blood could be members of the German nation — no Jews.

7 That foreigners should be deported if it was difficult to feed the people.

14 Profit-sharing in large industries.

15 More provision for old age.

16 Help for the middle class.

25 A strong central government.

Failure upon failure

The Beer-Hall Putsch

Hitler's first attempt to take power was a complete failure. In November 1923, in a Munich beer hall, Hitler jumped on a table and announced a 'National Revolution'. Flanked by a hero of the First World War, General Ludendorff, and followed by 3,000 Nazi storm troopers, Hitler set off on a march to Berlin. The Weimar Republic was in crisis and inflation was at its height. This was the moment to seize power, or so Hitler thought.

However, he did not have the police on his side. They blocked the marchers' route and during the shooting which followed, 16 Nazis and 3 policemen were killed.

Hitler was arrested, but was sentenced to only 5 years in prison. (He served 9 months.) The fact that someone received such a short sentence for trying to overthrow the Republic demonstrated how little respect there was for it. But this whole incident gave Hitler national publicity.

In Landsberg Prison he wrote *Mein Kampf* ('My Struggle'), which included page after page of his rantings about the Jews, the French, the Communists and many other objects of his scorn.

No progress

When Stresemann took over as Chancellor, the Weimar Republic began to recover (see page 42). As industrial production grew and wages increased (by one-third up to 1928), Hitler's extremism made little impact. In 1928 the Nazis gained only 12 seats in the Reichstag. They were clearly on the fringe of politics, as most people put their faith in moderate republican parties.

Hitler with four of his followers in the Landsberg Prison

How did Hitler become Chancellor?

Germany and the Depression

◆ The Wall Street Crash led to a Depression in Germany. As world trade collapsed, German factories began to close. American banks demanded the repayment of millions of dollars which had been lent to Germany following the Dawes Plan.
◆ Unemployment rose to record levels. By 1933, 6,000,000 Germans were out of work.
◆ The Weimar governments seemed incapable of taking action to reduce poverty. For example, the Social Democratic Party under Brüning was driven to object to cuts in social security payments.
◆ President Hindenburg, now over 80 years old, was forced to replace weak coalition governments with rule by decree. This was dangerous, as it meant that the Reichstag was not being consulted when important decisions were taken.

The rise of the Nazis

◆ In 1928, before the Depression, the Nazis had little support — only 12 seats in the Reichstag.
◆ As the Depression worsened, Germans looked for extreme solutions to their problems.
◆ They turned to the Nazis who, in 1930, secured 107 seats (to become the second largest party) and to the Communists who took 77 seats.

What did the Nazis offer?

Hitler portrayed himself as Germany's 'last hope'. He tried to offer every section of society something. He said a Nazi government would:
◆ make Germany powerful and recover lost pride
◆ destroy the humiliating Treaty of Versailles
◆ destroy the Jews and the Weimar government (to the Nazis they were scapegoats who could be blamed for all Germany's problems)
◆ offer jobs and military service to the unemployed
◆ boost rearmament orders for industrialists
◆ offer land and lower taxes to farmers
◆ destroy the Communist threat to the middle classes and property owners

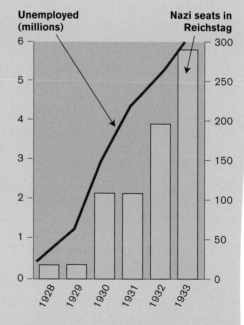

Nazi seats in the Reichstag and unemployment in Germany, 1928–33

Fear and propaganda

Hitler was the Nazis' greatest asset. He was a powerful public speaker, who made a dramatic impact on the thousands of people who went to his rallies. Under Goebbels the Nazis also developed propaganda techniques which won over many ordinary Germans — using posters, torchlight processions, mass rallies, film and radio.

For many still opposed to the Nazis, fear was used to silence them. Nazi storm troopers (the SA or 'Brown-shirts') beat up opponents, disrupted meetings held by Communists, harassed Jews and marched through the streets to show their strength.

Hitler makes a bid for power

After 1930, Nazi strength grew. Hitler had financial support from wealthy capitalists and was able to pay for expensive election campaigns. He even used aeroplanes to take his message to several parts of Germany in one day.

In 1932 Hitler challenged Hindenburg for the Presidency of Germany. Although he lost, Hitler proved his popularity by winning 13 million votes, against Hindenburg's 19 million. In July 1932 the Nazis won 230 seats in the Reichstag, making them the largest party. They dropped to 196 seats in November and the President managed to keep Hitler out of power — but for how long?

Political plots

At the end of 1932 the Chancellor, von Papen, was sacked. But he wanted to hold on to power and came up with a plan to regain control of the government. He persuaded the President to make Hitler Chancellor, with von Papen as Vice-Chancellor. In this way von Papen thought he could control Hitler. In January 1933 Hitler became Chancellor; but he had no intention of being upstaged or releasing his grip on power.

 Exam watch

Questions may focus on the growth of the Nazis and the reasons why Hitler became Chancellor.

*What were the early ideas of the Nazi Party in the 1920s and why did it grow so slowly up to 1930? How and why was Hitler able to become Chancellor in 1933? What was the relative importance of the different reasons why Hitler was able to become Chancellor? Think about the effects of the **First World War**, the **Treaty of Versailles**, the **weaknesses** of the Weimar Constitution and politicians, the effects of the Depression, the appeal of the Nazis, their **propaganda**, Nazi **violence**, and the actions of Hindenburg and von Papen. Was Hitler the Nazis' **most valuable asset**?*

How did Hitler become dictator of Germany in 1933–34?

Setting the scene

In January 1933 Hitler became Chancellor of Germany. The Nazis were only one party of many and Hitler was not firmly in control. However, by the end of 1934, Germany had become a one-party state, with Hitler its dictator. How did this happen?

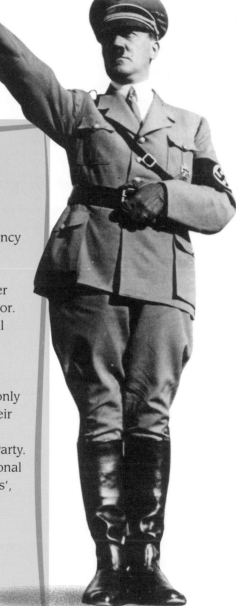

Key points

◆ Hitler called elections to increase his majority in the Reichstag (German parliament).
◆ On 27 February 1933 the Reichstag burned down.
◆ Hitler blamed the Communists. He asked for emergency powers to stop what he said was the start of a Communist revolution.
◆ The Enabling Law (March 1933) gave Hitler the power to pass laws by himself — he was becoming a dictator.
◆ Hitler and the Nazis set about banning other political parties, particularly the Communists.
◆ Trade unions were abolished.
◆ Newspapers were taken under Nazi control.
◆ Local government was controlled by the Nazis and only civil servants loyal to them were allowed to keep their jobs.
◆ Hitler destroyed rivals to his power inside the Nazi Party.
◆ The SA and its leaders were a threat to Hitler's personal power. In June 1934, on the 'Night of the Long Knives', SA leaders were killed by the SS.
◆ In August 1934, President Hindenburg died.
◆ Hitler assumed the title of President — then *Führer* (leader).
◆ The SS and the army gave a personal oath of loyalty to Hitler.

The Nazis, Nationalists and Centre Party voted together and the Communists were banned from the Reichstag. Members of other parties were threatened and attacked by Nazi supporters.

The Nazis were thus able to pass the **Enabling Law**.

Hitler was empowered to pass laws for four years, without interference from the Reichstag.

The Enabling Law brought the Weimar Constitution to an end and gave Hitler the means to become a dictator.

Winning people over to his side

Goebbels was in charge of propaganda. He ensured that Germans heard only the Nazi message, while anti-Nazi views were eliminated. Newspapers were controlled by the Ministry of Propaganda. In May 1933 books written by non-Nazi writers were burned in huge bonfires. Goebbels realised that the spoken word would have more impact than written news, so cheap radios were made available and loudspeakers were put up in the streets. Film makers had to have their work approved before it could be shown in cinemas.

At huge rallies, such as Nuremberg, thousands of Hitler's supporters flocked to hear him speak, giving the impression of Nazi strength and mass support. Hitler's greatest asset was his extraordinary power over mass audiences. His public speeches delivered an electrifying and overwhelming message to thousands of ordinary Germans, who were inspired with hope for the future.

Crushing the opposition, inside and outside the Nazi Party

As the key points show, Germany had become a one-party state. Regional parliaments were replaced by Nazi governors. Nazis took over all-important posts in local government, the courts, education, the police and the civil service.

Concentration camps such as Dachau (1933) were set up, run by the SS, (see page 53) to imprison leaders of trade unions and other political parties.

Hitler also had to eliminate rivals within the Nazi Party. Ernst Roehm was leader of the powerful SA (storm troopers). By 1934 they numbered 3,000,000. Roehm was ambitious and wanted to take over the army too. On 30 June 1934 (the Night of the Long Knives) Hitler's SS rounded up hundreds of the SA's leaders. Many, like Roehm, were shot and others arrested.

Only President Hindenburg now stood between Hitler and absolute power. When the old President died in August 1934, Hitler became sole leader of Germany. He immediately set about controlling life for ordinary Germans in all its aspects. Germany was to become a **totalitarian** state.

Exam watch

What steps did Hitler take to establish his dictatorship? What was the importance of the Enabling Law and the Night of the Long Knives? Who do you think was really responsible for the burning of the Reichstag?

How did Hitler keep control of the Nazi state?

The police state

In a totalitarian state, the government not only tries to control people's lives but also watches them to make sure its hold on power is never threatened. Fear was used to maintain control. How?

The SS (*Schutzstaffel* or 'Blackshirts') began as Hitler's bodyguard. After 1929 its leader, Heinrich Himmler, turned it into a powerful organisation of fanatical, élite Nazis. In 1934 it was used to eliminate the leaders of the SA (Brownshirts). It went on to spy on other Nazis, destroy all opposition, and carry out genocide against the Jews and gypsies. SS groups included the:

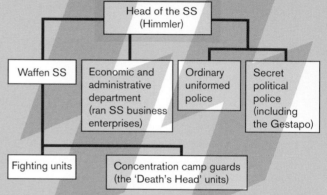

The structure of the SS

◆ **Gestapo** (secret police) which could imprison people without trial and send them to concentration camps, wielding unlimited power.
◆ **'Death's Head'** units which guarded concentration camps and ran the gas chambers.
◆ **Einsatzgruppen** (action squads) which killed Jews, gypsies, priests and anyone brave enough to oppose the Nazis in occupied lands.
◆ **Waffen SS**, an armed force which fought alongside the German army.

Concentration camps were started in 1933. At first they were just old buildings converted into prisons for Hitler's enemies: Communists, trade union leaders and socialists. Later special camps were built for Jews, priests, gypsies and other groups targeted by the SS. Only after 1941 did some of these become death camps to exterminate Jews and other persecuted peoples.

Police and courts were under SS control. Police forces were run by Nazis and all judges had to be loyal members of the party. Spies and informers were everywhere, and it was impossible for opponents of the regime to get a fair trial. The cruel activities of SS members were outside the law, so they not only went unpunished but were encouraged.

Propaganda

Dr Josef Goebbels, who became Minister of Public Enlightenment, aimed to encourage people to support Hitler and, after 1933, to make them into good Nazis. Information was strictly controlled; Germans were allowed to hear only about Nazi strengths and successes.

The media

- Anti-Nazi newspapers were closed and their editors sacked.
- Cheap radios were made available to ensure that the Nazi message reached many homes.
- Loudspeakers were installed in public areas.
- Films, many of them made by the best directors, publicised Nazi achievements or policies.
- In 1933 Goebbels set up the Reich Chamber of Culture. Any artist who wanted to publish a play or book, make a film, write a piece of music, etc. had to be a member.
- In May 1933 books with which the Nazis disagreed were publicly burned.
- Jazz was banned — as black music, it was considered inferior.

Rallies and parades

Giant parades, marches, rallies and torch-light processions were staged to show off Nazi power and support. Each September the Nuremberg rally took place. People were excited by these huge, stage-managed gatherings; they were made to feel part of a strong movement, which was giving Germans back their pride. The Nazis appeared to be organised, powerful, successful. At the climax, Hitler would appear. His effect on audiences was electric. He had the ability to brainwash people into becoming Nazis.

The 1936 Olympic Games

The Berlin games were used for propaganda. A new stadium was built to impress visitors from abroad. Germany came top of the medal table, although the hero of the games (to Hitler's fury) was the American, Jesse Owens, who won four gold medals. He was not an Aryan but a black athlete — to the Nazis, 'a member of an inferior race'.

Young people

Schools were run by Nazis. Physical education was the most important subject. History textbooks emphasised stories about the hated French, the despised Jews and Weimar politicians, the 'disease from the East' (Communism) and why it was important to destroy the Treaty of Versailles. In biology, Nazi racial ideas were taught and eugenics, the theory of the pure Aryan race. In chemistry children were taught about chemical warfare, and in maths about ballistics.

The Hitler Youth (boys) and the **League of German Maidens** (girls) were organisations for young Germans between the ages of 10 and 18. Boys would march in parades and be brainwashed by Nazi ideas. Girls were taught parenthood, biology and domestic science. They would be mothers of the future 'master race' and their first loyalty was to be to the Führer, not their parents. They, too, were indoctrinated and prepared for the 'Thousand Year Reich'.

By 1938 two-thirds of all young people had joined the Nazi Party. In 1939 membership was made compulsory. Germany's future was being secured for the Nazis.

BERLIN 1936
16 AUG

OLYMPISCHE SPIEL

Nazi ideas in action

Racial policies

Anti-Semitism is hatred of Jews. Hitler blamed them for all Germany's problems. They were the scapegoat for every disaster — defeat, reparations, the Depression, unemployment and so on. In fact, Jews made up only 1% of the population and most lived quite ordinary lives. Some were well off, but many were not. Hitler's ideas about them were myths. Jews were portrayed as money lenders, who lived apart from the rest of society. Propaganda spread the impression that they were vermin which infested Germany. Ordinary Germans were made jealous — the Jews were portrayed as having the best jobs and the most prosperous businesses. Jews were an easy target, with little chance of defending themselves and a long history of discrimination against them.

Other minority groups were also persecuted. Homosexuals were sent to concentration camps, as they did not conform to the Nazi ideal of family life. People who were mentally ill were gassed or given lethal injections, as they might weaken the Aryan master race. Women who carried hereditary illnesses were forcibly sterilised. Gypsies were also regarded as 'sub-human' and the majority of them went to the gas chambers.

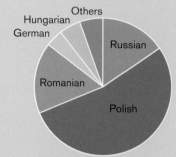

The total number of victims was approximately 6 million

The nationalities of the victims of the Holocaust

Persecution

The first steps

As early as April 1933, Hitler ordered the boycott of Jewish shops, businesses, doctors and lawyers. Their properties were marked with the Star of David and SA men were posted outside. Jews were sacked from jobs in the media, the civil service and teaching.

The Nuremberg Laws

From 1935 these laws, sometimes known as the Reich Citizenship laws, prevented Jews from gaining German citizenship. Jews could not vote or hold official posts. They were forbidden to have sexual relations with 'pure' Germans, according to the Blood Protection Act. Mixed marriages were immediately barred. Jews became 'outcasts' in German society. As a result, by 1937 half the Jewish population had left the country; of those who remained, many had lost their jobs and their savings.

Kristallnacht

In early November 1938, a German official in Paris was murdered by a Jewish student. This was just the excuse the Nazis wanted. The SS triggered off the 'Night of Broken Glass', a vicious attack on Jewish property and synagogues — 90 Jews died and over 20,000 were rounded up and sent to concentration camps. The Jewish community was fined 1 billion marks for the murder.

The Final Solution

In 1942 Hitler invaded the USSR and millions of Jews came under Nazi control. What would they do with them? Eventually Hitler and Himmler came up with the 'Final Solution' — genocide. The SS set up death camps such as Auschwitz and Treblinka, where Jews and others were exploited, used as slave labour, or gassed. Six million died in this 'Holocaust' (destruction). When the Jews fought back — for example, in the Warsaw rising of 1944 — the Nazis dealt with them with horrific violence.

Hitler never had a clear plan from the beginning about how to deal with the Jews. The policy emerged piece by piece. Only 2 million Jews were left in Europe after the Holocaust.

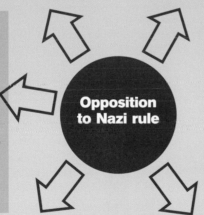

1 **Communists** and **socialists** were implacable opponents, but most of their leaders ended up in concentration camps in 1933 and 1934.

2 Hitler encouraged Nazi Protestants to join his 'Reich Church'. *Mein Kampf* replaced the Bible. A sword replaced the cross. Only Nazi preachers were allowed. Pagan worship called the Faith Movement was also encouraged.

However, powerful opposition came from the **Church**. There was an obvious clash between Nazi beliefs and the Christian message of charity and love. Many Protestant churchmen ended up in concentration camps. Two famous ones were Pastor Niemöller, who was incarcerated from 1938 to 1945, and Dietrich Bonhoeffer, who organised opposition to Hitler. He asked the Allies for peace terms if Hitler was overthrown! He paid for this with his life — he was hanged before the end of the war.

5 Other anti-Hitler movements sprang up amongst the **young**, who became tired of strict rules and constant military drill. Two of these were the 'Swing' movement and the 'Edelweiss Pirates'.

Opposition to Nazi rule

4 Otherwise the most famous example of opposition was the July 1944 **bomb plot** by leading **army officers**. The bomb went off, but Hitler survived. 5,000 others didn't — they were executed as a punishment. Many of these opponents were from the German upper classes, which despised Nazi greed and cruelty.

3 The **Catholic Church** too caused some trouble, but Hitler signed an agreement with the Pope to keep him out of politics. He promised to leave the Church alone if the Pope did not interfere in Nazi affairs. This agreement was called the **Concordat**. Some Roman Catholic priests continued to preach against Nazi violence. Cardinal Innitzer had his church smashed. Hundreds of priests still ended up in concentration camps.

How did the Nazis change people's lives?

Work and the economy

The problem

- The economic crisis of the early 1930s meant 6 million were unemployed in 1933.

- Many workers did not support the Nazis.

- Germany needed to organise the economy to pay for the expansion of the armed forces.

- Hitler was concerned that Germany was not self-sufficient in goods, so he wished to reduce imports and boost exports.

Nazi solutions

1 The workers

In 1933 trade unions were outlawed. They were replaced by the *Deutsche Arbeitsfront* (DAF) — the German Labour Front. Strikes were banned and employers and employees were encouraged to work together in the interests of the state.

2 The National Labour Service

All 18–25 year olds undertook 6 months' compulsory labour service. Men worked on building projects. Slums were cleared, *autobahns* (motorways) were built and sports facilities expanded. Pay was low and hours long.

3 Expansion

Nazi bureaucracy and the expansion of industries related to rearmament meant many of the unemployed found work. Hitler claimed to have solved the unemployment problem. Whether or not compulsory labour is a solution to 'real' unemployment continues to be argued about.

4 'Strength through Joy'

This policy attempted to win over workers by providing sports, cultural and recreational facilities, as well as cheap holidays. It persuaded people to pay money into a scheme which would eventually enable them to buy one of the new 'people's cars' (Volkswagen). None in fact were delivered; when war came, the factory was converted to weapons production.

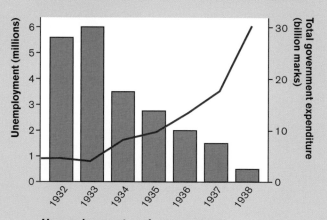

Unemployment and government expenditure in Germany, 1932–38

Women and the Nazi state

- The Nazi Party had a traditional view of women, summed up as: 'Kinder, Kirche und Küche' (children, church and cooking). Their role was at home, supporting their husbands and having children — to feed future German armies. The ideal woman had a large family and gave up her job to make way for a man.
- Consequently, male unemployment would fall and as the German population grew, so would the Nazi state. Women won medals for producing large families — a gold 'Mother Cross' for having eight children! Couples also received loans when they got married.
- Women in employment were discriminated against when applying for jobs. Those in employment were often either forced out or bribed to give up work, with the offer of generous social security benefits. Medicine, the law and the civil service were to become occupations reserved for men.
- The birth rate rose and male unemployment fell. Nazi planners even found themselves short of labour. Women had to be brought back into the factories, particularly during the war when armaments were desperately required. However, despite mounting losses in the armed forces, few women were allowed to join.

The role of women in Nazi Germany

Autarky and Lebensraum

Hitler's aim of self-sufficiency for Germany (called autarky) meant two things:

◆ *Lebensraum* was the expansion of Germany into new 'living-space' — territory to the east, where Germany could seize wheat-growing land and areas which could be exploited for oil.

◆ The development of ersatz (or synthetic) materials, such as artificially produced rubber and wool, was vigorously pursued. Nazi scientists and engineers put much effort into producing synthetic replacements for materials which had to be imported and which were vulnerable in time of war.

During the **Second World War** Germans faced:

◆ rationing and shortages of food and clothing
◆ lack of medical facilities
◆ the impact of 'total war', as non-essential production was stopped and everything was geared towards the war effort
◆ a severe refugee problem
◆ the effects of bombing raids on German cities and, in 1945, invasion

Map showing the British bombing of German cities, 1940–45

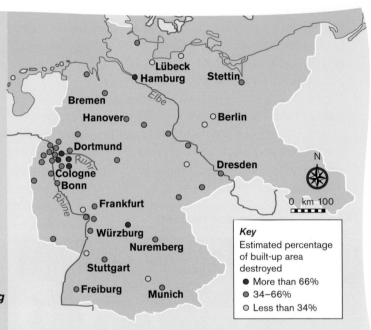

Key
Estimated percentage of built-up area destroyed
● More than 66%
◑ 34–66%
○ Less than 34%

What happened when the tide of war turned against Hitler?

In the years 1939 to 1941, Hitler's armies conquered large areas of Europe and goods inside Germany were not in short supply. However, heavy bombing of German cities and defeats by the Soviet army on the Eastern Front began to drain the Nazi state of resources. Censorship became very strict and civilians faced terrible sacrifices. In 1942, Albert Speer became armaments minister and Germany geared itself up for 'total war'. By 1945, Germans were scavenging for food and searching for shelter in bombed-out cities. On 30 April Hitler committed suicide and in May Germany finally surrendered.

 Exam watch

*Concentrate on learning the main features of Hitler's totalitarian state. These were: **control** — the one-party state, the use of fear and persecution, the treatment of the young, propaganda and censorship, the use of education, the SS and Gestapo and how the Nazis dealt with the opposition; **racial policies** — and how these changed over time. What were the effects of Nazi policies on the German people? Did they benefit at any time from them?*

The rise and fall
of the USSR
1914–90

Background to the Russian Revolution

Before 1914, there were huge extremes of wealth in Russia. The industrialisation of the country was just beginning and there was massive population growth in places such as St Petersburg and Moscow. Some 80% of the population, however, were peasants and most of these were illiterate.

The Tsar had absolute power, which meant that he could make laws, appoint ministers and decide on all policies completely on his own. He had ministers to advise him, but he did not have to heed their advice. The army could be used to frighten opponents and suppress revolt, and the secret police (Okhrana) ensured that all serious opposition was stamped on.

Ruling class
(royal family and government) 1%

Upper class
(nobles, leading church officials, senior officers and civil servants) 12%

Commercial class
(bankers, merchants, factory owners) 1%

Working class 4%

Peasants 82%

Russia's social classes

Tsar Nicholas II was a weak character. He was dominated by his wife and he did not relish the task of running the country. As war approached, he failed to act decisively.

◆ In 1905, there had been a revolution in Russia and Nicholas had promised to make changes to the way the country was run. Most of the promises were broken or ignored, and by 1914 opposition to the Tsar was growing again.

◆ When war came, Nicholas failed to understand the seriousness of the situation in Russia and went off to supervise his armies, leaving his wife, Alexandra, in charge of the day-to-day running of the country. Alexandra, however, was under the influence of Rasputin, a devious and unscrupulous man who had secured his place at court because he was able to heal the Tsar's son, who suffered from haemophilia.

The Tsar and Tsarina in the hands of the notorious Rasputin

Opposition groups before 1914

There were many opposition groups in Russia:

◆ The biggest group was the **Socialist Revolutionaries**. They were supported largely by disaffected peasants.

◆ But the Social Democrats eventually became the most significant. In 1903 they split in two: **Bolsheviks** and **Mensheviks**. They drew their support from the big cities such as St Petersburg and Moscow.

Both these groups wanted to overthrow the Tsar.

Other political groups were the **Kadets** and the **Octobrists**. The Octobrists were formed after the 1905 Revolution. They were happy to retain the monarchy, but they failed to change the way the country was run.

The impact of the First World War

As in most other countries in 1914, there was great support for the war when it started. Despite this optimism, however, the Russians were soon defeated by the Germans, and the Russian army was seen to be inefficient and poorly equipped. Soldiers often went into action with no rifles and were told to take them from those who had been killed.

Russian infantry during general mobilisation, 1914

In 1915 Nicholas appointed himself Commander-in-Chief, but the war went badly for Russia. At home things were no better:

◆ The railway system was inadequate and soon broke down.

There was plenty of food, but not enough locomotives to pull the trains and this led to severe shortages. The worst affected places were St Petersburg (now renamed Petrograd) and Moscow.

◆ Food shortages led to inflation. In Petrograd prices of many foodstuffs rose by 300%.

◆ Alexandra ran the government under the influence of Rasputin. They sacked ministers who did not agree with them and often appointed others who were weak and inexperienced.

◆ Rumours spread about the influence of Rasputin and his relationship with the Tsarina. He was murdered in 1916 by a group of Russian nobles.

 Exam watch

Remember to focus on errors made by the Tsar before 1914, broken promises and then the impact of the war. Note: Rasputin is an important factor, but do not write irrelevancies about him.

Why were there two revolutions in 1917?

As the war progressed, the royal family became increasingly unpopular. The Tsarina and her government were seen as weak and corrupt. Rasputin was despised — and eventually murdered.

Tsar Nicholas and his family

Food prices rose as food grew scarce and queues became commonplace. Moreover, the Tsar was unable to secure any military victories. In February there were demonstrations and parades. A large number of workers went on strike in Petrograd. The intensity of the strikes and demonstrations increased and, when troops were sent to stop the unrest, the garrison of Petrograd supported the strikers. The February Revolution was under way:

- The workers began to form councils to organise their work and other activities. (These became known as **soviets**.)
- Leaders of the Duma (the parliament in Petrograd) began to oppose the Tsar. When he tried to return to take charge of the government, it was too late. Troops joined the rioters and on 2 March Nicholas abdicated.
- A **Provisional Government** was then set up.

Problems of the Provisional Government

The Provisional Government was a temporary government created by members of the Duma until a general election could be held. The first prime minister was Prince Lvov, who was replaced by Alexander Kerensky in July 1917.

The Provisional Government:

- continued the war against Germany, because it did not wish to let the Western Allies down. Continuing the war lost the support of many ordinary Russian citizens

- did little to solve the land problem for the peasants and, above all, it did not work harmoniously with the Petrograd Soviet

- failed to solve issues such as inflation, poor working conditions and low wages

The **Petrograd Soviet** was elected by the soldiers and workers of Petrograd. It governed Petrograd and was controlled at first by the Socialist Revolutionaries. It issued Military Order Number One which stated that orders from the Provisional Government were only to be obeyed if they were approved by the Soviet.

The Bolshevik rise to power and the October Revolution

Lenin, the exiled leader of the Bolsheviks, returned to Petrograd in April 1917 and published the *April Theses*. Lenin offered 'peace, land and bread' to the Russian people. Revolution was brewing again:

◆ In **May** and **July** the Bolsheviks tried to seize power in Petrograd, but failed. Lenin fled.

◆ In **August** the army commander-in-chief, General Kornilov, challenged Kerensky, wanting to impose a much stricter regime. As the army marched on Petrograd, Kerensky asked the Bolsheviks to help him. They were given weapons and they stopped Kornilov's advance — and then refused to give up their arms.

◆ In **October** Lenin returned and convinced the Bolsheviks that they could seize power.

◆ A leading Bolshevik, **Leon Trotsky**, organised cutting of telephone wires and seizing control of the post office, railway stations and other key buildings. Bolshevik troops stormed the Winter Palace, where the Provisional Government met. The army did not come to its assistance.

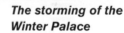

The storming of the Winter Palace

The Bolshevik Revolution had succeeded, but it had secured Petrograd only. The Bolsheviks now had to fight to win control of the whole of Russia.

🞂 Exam watch

Focus on the spontaneous nature of February 1917. Do not forget to analyse the errors made by the Provisional Government. Concentrate too on the simple appeal of the Bolsheviks.

Lenin's direct appeal to the Russian people

The Bolshevik Revolution and the Civil War

Land lost in the Treaty of Brest-Litovsk

Russia lost:

62 million people (one sixth of the population)

27% of farmland (some of the best in Russia)

26% of railways

74% of iron ore and coal

Map of the settlement of the Treaty of Brest-Litovsk

0   km   1,000

The Provisional Government was replaced by a Council of the People's Commissars, but Lenin was determined that the Bolsheviks should consolidate their hold on power.

◆ He issued the Peace Decree, which ended the war with Germany. A Land Decree declared that land belonged to the peasants who farmed it. Businesses were taken over.

◆ A general election was held, in which the Socialist Revolutionaries won most of the seats. However, when the Constituent Assembly met in January 1918, Lenin dissolved it.

◆ In March 1918 the **Treaty of Brest-Litovsk** was signed with Germany. Russia surrendered a quarter of its land and people, but was no longer at war. Lenin could concentrate on consolidating the Revolution.

By the summer of 1918 Lenin, now ruling as a dictator, had many opponents — and civil war broke out.

Soldiers of the White Army executed by the Red Army

Why were the Bolsheviks successful in the Civil War?

◆ Their opponents, the Whites, were divided and never worked together properly.

◆ The White Russian forces numbered about 250,000. The Red Army eventually had 2 million men and controlled the centre of the country and the railway network.

◆ At first the Western Allies sent men and aid to the Whites, to oppose the Communist threat; but this was never enough and the Allies pulled out in 1919.

What was War Communism?

In May 1918 Lenin introduced the grain monopoly. All surplus grain became the property of the state.

All factories also became state property and whatever was produced was taken by the state. The workers were given rations in return.

War Communism was imposed by the CHEKA (secret police) and opponents were killed.

What were the effects of War Communism?

◆ By 1921 there was a famine, in which about 5 million people died, brought on as peasants refused to hand over their surpluses. Food production fell as peasants destroyed crops and killed animals, rather than surrender them.
◆ Uprisings spread. In the Kronstadt Mutiny, sailors who had been leading supporters of the Bolsheviks rebelled against War Communism. This finally proved to Lenin that the system was not working.

'Have you volunteered for the Red Army?' A Moscow political poster, 1920

The New Economic Policy

By 1921 it was clear that the Russian economy had collapsed (see table). Something new had to be tried — the New Economic Policy. So state ownership was relaxed. Peasants could now keep and sell their agricultural surpluses, and privately-owned small businesses could trade for profit.

The Russian economy slowly began to recover.

	1913	1922	1925
Output of coal (million tons)	29.0	9.5	18.1
Output of pig iron (million tons)	4.2	0.1	1.5
Grain harvest (million tons)	80.1	50.3	72.5
Cattle produced (million head)	58.9	45.8	62.1
Pigs produced (million head)	20.3	12.0	21.8

Industrial and agricultural recovery under the NEP

 **Exam watch**

Focus on why the Bolsheviks were successful in the Civil War, why the policy of War Communism failed, and the success of the New Economic Policy.

Stalin and the Five Year Plans

The emergence of Stalin

When Lenin died, he named Trotsky as his successor and recommended that Stalin should be dismissed as General Secretary of the Communist Party. However, some Bolshevik leaders saw Trotsky as arrogant and did not want him as leader.

◆ As General Secretary, Stalin wielded much power and influence.

◆ From 1924 the Soviet Union was ruled by a committee of Kamenev, Zinoviev and Stalin.

◆ Stalin played off the other Bolshevik leaders against each other and by 1928 they were no longer a threat to him.

Joseph Stalin

Why were the Plans introduced?

◆ Stalin believed that Soviet industry and agriculture was one hundred years behind the West. He said that they must catch up in 10 years.

◆ Stalin turned away from world revolution. He set out to create 'socialism in one country'.

◆ He distrusted Western Europe. Russia had been invaded in 1919 during the Civil War, and he wished to guard against future invasions.

◆ He wanted to replace the New Economic Policy, which Lenin had intended to be a temporary measure. Moreover, Stalin hated the Kulaks (land-owning peasants) and wanted to destroy them.

◆ In the first Five Year Plan, Stalin called for huge increases in the output of heavy industry.

How the Plans worked

◆ Private businesses were banned.

◆ GOSPLAN was set up. This central bureaucracy worked out targets for the production of all kinds of goods.

◆ Every factory throughout the Soviet Union was given targets and new industrial cities were created.

◆ Slave labour was used to help meet targets. People arrested in the Purges were sent to the gulag (labour camps), which were set up in the north and in Siberia. The inmates were often worked to death in appalling conditions.

◆ 'Stakhanovites' were created, named after Alexei Stakhanov, the coal miner. He was supposed to have dug more than 100 tonnes of coal in a single shift. All workers were urged to follow his example.

The appalling conditions of a Siberian labour camp

Problems with the Plans

- Few consumer goods were produced and safety standards were often non-existent.
- Most targets were ridiculously high and the quality of many goods was poor.
- The illiterate workforce often did not know how to operate machinery or mend it.
- Managers of factories falsified production records to hide their failures.
- Stalin would permit no criticism of the Plans.

Despite their weaknesses, huge increases in industrial production were achieved. By 1941 the USSR was the second strongest industrial power in the world behind the USA.

The population of the USSR grew substantially in the 1930s, but the numbers living in towns and cities grew more rapidly, reflecting the forced pace of industrialisation.

Exam watch

Questions often focus on why Stalin ended the New Economic Policy and introduced the Five Year Plans. You must be aware of the success/failure of the Plans.

Year	Total population	Total living in towns and cities	
1926	147.0 million	26.3 million	(18% of total)
1939	170.6 million	56.1 million	(33% of total)

Population growth and urbanisation, 1926 and 1939

	1927–28	Target for 1933	Actual for 1933
Coal	35.4	75.0	64.0
Oil	11.7	21.7	21.4
Pig iron	3.2	10.0	6.2

Industrial output of the First Five Year Plan, 1928–33 (million tonnes)

	1932	Target for 1937	Actual for 1937
Coal	64.0	152.5	128.0
Oil	21.4	46.8	28.5
Pig iron	6.2	16.0	14.5

Industrial output of the Second Five Year Plan, 1932–37 (million tonnes)

Changes under Stalin

Sacking the first grain harvest on a collective farm in the Ukraine, 1929

Collectivisation of agriculture

◆ Collectivisation was an attempt to get rid of the ownership of land by ordinary people. In particular, Stalin wanted to sell wheat abroad to raise foreign exchange, in order to buy new technology to help with the Five Year Plans.

Agricultural production in Russia, 1928–35

The figures are Western estimates based on Soviet statistics

Year	1928	1929	1930	1931	1932	1933	1934	1935
Grain (million tonnes)	73.3	71.7	83.5	69.5	69.6	68.6	67.6	75.0
Cattle (millions)	70.5	67.1	52.5	47.9	40.7	38.4	42.4	49.3
Pigs (millions)	26.0	20.4	13.6	14.4	11.6	12.1	17.4	22.6
Sheep and goats (millions)	146.7	147.0	108.8	77.7	52.1	50.2	51.9	61.1

Was collectivisation a success?

◆ Most peasants could not use the machinery that was supplied. Many tractors did not work.

◆ Large numbers of kulaks resisted and destroyed crops and animals. This led to a massive famine in 1932–34, in which some 5 million people died.

◆ By 1937, when collectivisation was almost complete, wheat production was up by a third on the 1928 figure.

◆ It was also an attempt to solve the food problem in the Soviet Union. Food rationing was introduced in 1928.
◆ Stalin wanted to destroy the kulaks, who enjoyed some independence and did not agree with his policies.
◆ Two types of collective farm were set up:
 ● the **sovkhoz**, or state farm, where all the land was owned by the state, all the produce went to the state, and workers were paid wages
 ● the **kolkhoz**, or collective farm, where workers were also allowed to keep some plots of land for themselves

These new farms were supplied by the state with tools, tractors, seeds etc.

Industrial growth, 1913–37

Coal — Million tonnes

1913 1921 1927-8 1932 1937 (approx.)

Steel — Million tonnes

1913 1921 1927-8 1932 1937 (approx.)

Oil — Million tonnes

1913 1921 1927-8 1932 1937 (approx.)

The effects of change on the Soviet people

On the face of it, the results were impressive, but there were also many disturbing developments during the 1930s.

There were **advantages...**
- Education and housing improved, and literacy increased rapidly.
- The number of doctors increased and medical treatment became more widely available.
- Industrial workers were given higher pay and rewarded with medals. Some social security benefits were provided.

But there were also **disadvantages...**
- A seven-day working week was introduced. Absence from work became a crime and skilled workers were not allowed to leave their jobs.
- Pay did not always keep up with the rise in prices, and living standards fell.
- The secret police were used to force people to accept change. Those who opposed the regime or protested found themselves in slave labour camps (the gulag). Dissidents were sentenced to work there for ten years or more, in harsh conditions with little food.
- During the **Purges**, many people were executed or sent to the gulag and never returned. It is not known how many disappeared. Estimates vary between 7 million and 20 million.

 Exam watch

Questions will frequently ask why collectivisation was introduced and then move on to the opposition — what form it took and why. When you revise, ask yourself these questions.

Stalin's dictatorship

The Purges

In the 1930s Stalin began to get rid of anyone whom he suspected of opposing him. This process became known as the Purges.

At first the Purges concentrated on technical experts, whom Stalin blamed for the failures of the first Five Year Plan. They were accused of sabotage and there was a series of trials in 1930–31. The purging escalated rapidly:

◆ In 1932 more than 800,000 members of the party were expelled, but the real purges began with the murder of Sergei Kirov in 1934. He was the Communist Party leader in Leningrad and he was probably murdered on Stalin's orders because he was a rival.

Sergei Kirov

◆ The Purges lasted from 1934 to 1938; at least 7 million people disappeared. Bolshevik leaders, poets, writers, artists and musicians were all targeted for holding to ideas which Stalin did not like.

◆ Managers of industries who did not meet their production targets were also victims, as were scientists, engineers and experts of every kind. The military were particularly singled out: every Admiral of the Soviet fleet, three of the five Marshals of the Red Army, 90% of its Generals and more than half of its other officers were purged. The purging of the armed forces proved disastrous in the first two years of the war against Germany.

◆ Millions of ordinary Soviet citizens were also purged, often not even knowing what they had done to anger Stalin.

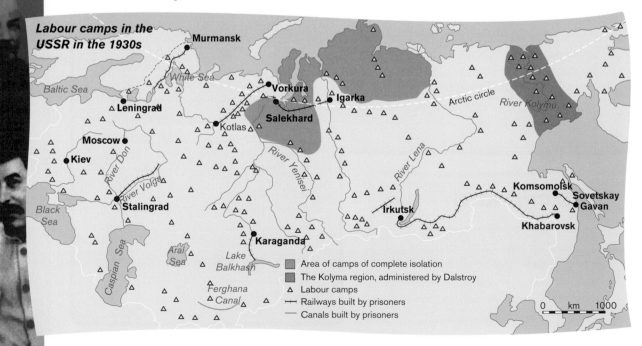

Labour camps in the USSR in the 1930s

- ■ Area of camps of complete isolation
- ■ The Kolyma region, administered by Dalstroy
- △ Labour camps
- ⊢⊢ Railways built by prisoners
- — Canals built by prisoners

The Show Trials

The leading Bolsheviks were given 'Show Trials'. They were accused of sabotage and treason and of murdering Kirov — often crimes that they could not possibly have committed. The aim was to get rid of all the Old Bolsheviks, who knew the truth about Lenin and Stalin. They all confessed to the crimes of which they were accused, usually because they were told that their families would be left alone if they did.

The results of the trials were announced to the world. Altogether, 35 of the leading Old Bolsheviks were executed in 1936–38.

The Cult of Personality

Stalin decided to build himself up to be all-powerful and to stop anyone opposing his ideas. He made himself out to be an infallible and superior being. This became known as the 'Cult of Personality'. He reinforced it in a number of ways:

◆ Stalin created the impression that he was a genius at everything. He was described as the 'wisest man of the twentieth century', the 'genius of the age'. The Soviet people were told that he was never wrong. This protected Stalin from any further challenges.

◆ He expected love and worship, not respect and obedience. He made sure that everyone knew about his successes. Huge rallies were held in his honour.

◆ He used many forms of propaganda, but his favourites were painting and sculpture. Images of Stalin appeared all over Russia. They showed him meeting smiling people, opening factories, dams etc; and he always looked rather taller and fitter than he actually was.

Exam watch

Ensure you know thoroughly the props of Stalin's power — the Purges, the cult of personality etc. You must be able to explain each carefully.

The Leningrad Parade, July 1935

Stalin and the Second World War

Response to invasion

The German invasion of the Soviet Union in 1941 led to a string of defeats for the Red Army. German troops penetrated deep into the Russian heartland and the country found itself fighting for its very existence. Stalin realised that drastic steps must be taken to avoid conquest by Germany.

◆ He ordered the countryside to be destroyed as the Red Army retreated. Everything was burned or laid to waste in order to deny the enemy any help or sustenance.

◆ He appealed to Soviet citizens to defend the motherland to their last breath.

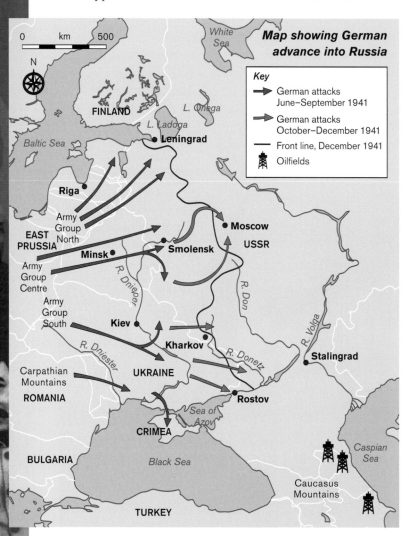

Map showing German advance into Russia

Key
→ German attacks June–September 1941
→ German attacks October–December 1941
— Front line, December 1941
⛏ Oilfields

Whole factories, and even towns, were moved further east, out of the reach of the German armies.

Stalin left military matters to his generals, particularly Marshal Zhukov.

Marshal Zhukov

Stalin remained in the Kremlin to convince the Soviet people that he believed the Soviet Union would win in the end. He called the war the 'Great Patriotic War'. An enormous amount of propaganda was produced to urge the Soviet people to fight.

After the war

Stalin was involved in conferences to shape the postwar world, at Yalta and Potsdam, but he did not trust the Western Allies and turned his back on them. The USSR set up Communist governments in the countries of Eastern Europe which had been overrun by Soviet troops as they pursued the defeated German armies. Germany was divided and the Soviet Union retreated into isolation behind the 'Iron Curtain'.

◆ Stalin died in 1953 and was mourned as a national hero.

◆ Following his death, Malenkov became Prime Minister; the new Secretary of the Communist Party was Nikita Khrushchev.

◆ From 1953 to 1955 the Soviet Union was governed by a committee composed of Malenkov, Molotov, Khrushchev and Bulganin. By 1956 it was clear that Khrushchev was the man in power.

Effects of the war on the Soviet Union

The war between Germany and the Soviet Union was exceedingly bitter. Victory was secured only with the help of the Western Allies and at enormous cost.

◆ 1,710 towns, 70,000 villages and 84,000 schools were destroyed. At least 20 million people in the Soviet Union lost their lives. By the end of the war, 25 million Russians were homeless.

◆ Most of European Russia was destroyed and many of the advances of the 1930s were wiped out.

Exam watch

Focus on the How *and* Why *behind the USSR's survival.*

Key dates in Stalin's life

1879	Born in Tiflis, Georgia
1910	Member of Bolshevik Central Committee
1913	Exiled to Turukhansk
1918	Commissar for Nationalities
1919	General Secretary of the Communist Party
1924	Led the Soviet Union with Zinoviev and Kamenev after death of Lenin
1929	By this time Trotsky was exiled and the Left/Right had been removed
1934	Purges began
1953	Death of Stalin

Russian leaders flank the open coffin of Joseph Stalin, March 1953

The USSR under Khrushchev

Nikita Khrushchev

The policy of de-Stalinisation

In 1956 Khrushchev attacked Stalin in the 'secret speech'. He branded him a dictator and an enemy of the people.

Although the practice of religion was controlled and the number of churches reduced, more freedom was given to writers and artists. Alexander Solzhenitsyn's book, *One Day in the Life of Ivan Denisovich*, which criticised the labour camps, was allowed to be published. Solzhenitsyn had himself been imprisoned in a gulag.

A less harsh regime, and a rejection of the Stalin cult, was indicated in other ways:

◆ Khrushchev did not eliminate his rivals, as Stalin had done. They were given unimportant jobs instead.

◆ Stalingrad was renamed Volgograd. Other towns, villages and streets were renamed.

◆ The power of the secret police was curtailed. The gulags were closed and millions of political prisoners were released.

◆ In 1960 Stalin's body was removed from the Lenin Mausoleum in Moscow's Red Square.

Changes in agriculture

Khrushchev believed that he was an expert and would not listen to advice. He continually interfered, with disastrous results:

◆ He set up collective farms in Kazakhstan (the Virgin Lands scheme) to solve the problems of Soviet agriculture. But the Virgin Lands could not support wheat for more than a few years; too little money was spent on fertiliser. By 1960 the Virgin Lands scheme had failed. In 1962 bad weather washed away most of the topsoil and the Virgin Lands were ruined forever.

◆ There was no way of transporting the crops. Kazakhstan was too remote and the railway network was inefficient.

◆ Many other farms were forced to grow maize, which Khrushchev believed would provide fodder for animals and release grain for human consumption. The climate in the Soviet Union was not suitable for growing maize, but Khrushchev refused to listen to advice.

Changes in industry

Khrushchev wanted to show that the Soviet Union could be as successful as the USA. He encouraged the production of more consumer goods. But the resources necessary for this were being swallowed up by the Soviet space programme.

He also set up Regional Economic Councils to control different areas of the country and encouraged them to make their own decisions. But the Regional Councils were a failure because their managers did not believe that they had real authority. Everyone was used to being told what to do, as they had been under Stalin.

The fall of Khrushchev

None of Khrushchev's promises to his people was kept. There was some improvement in living standards, but there were still shortages of food and most other items.

He was seen as having been humiliated over the Cuban Missile Crisis and some colleagues felt that he had gone too far in his attacks on Stalin. They believed he was encouraging too much criticism and he fell from power in 1964.

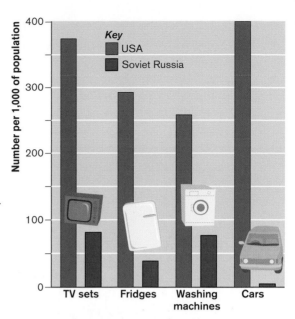

Ownership of consumer goods in the mid-1960s

Exam watch

Questions tend to focus on why Khrushchev introduced de-Stalinisation and also on what Khrushchev's policies were. Concentrate on causation and change.

The end of the Communist state

The Brezhnev era

Khrushchev was succeeded by Leonid Brezhnev, who was opposed to the notion of change. The Soviet Union went through a period of stagnation and repression, when liberal-minded writers and thinkers were again imprisoned. Brezhnev began to spend more on the arms race, because he believed that the Soviet Union had fallen behind the USA in the **Cold War**.

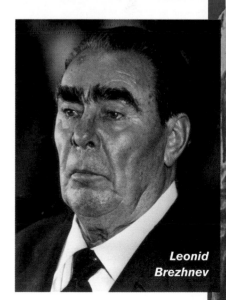

Leonid Brezhnev

This expenditure drained the Soviet economy, which was failing because:

◆ There was serious corruption in government. Brezhnev promoted members of his own family to senior posts.

◆ Agricultural problems got worse and food shortages were common. The Soviet Union was unable to produce enough wheat to feed its population and had to import from the USA. There was little incentive for peasants to work hard and investment in new technology was non-existent.

Soviet tanks in Afghanistan

In 1979 the Soviet Union invaded Afghanistan. It tried to support the Communist government against Muslim rebels. The cost of the war was enormous.

In 1981 Brezhnev blamed the failures of the tenth Five Year Plan on a lack of skilled labour, alcoholism, absenteeism and lack of effort on the part of civil servants.

Brezhnev died in 1982 and was succeeded by Yuri Andropov. However, Andropov died in 1984 and was replaced by Konstantin Chernenko. He was seventy-two and in poor health and died in 1985. This time a younger man was chosen — Mikhail Gorbachev.

 Exam watch

Be prepared to answer why the Soviet Union was in such a mess by the 1980s and make sure you are able to define perestroika *and* glasnost. *You should also be able to explain why Gorbachev failed.*

Gorbachev saw **perestroika** as 'economic restructuring'. He believed that the Soviet Union could survive only if the economy was radically reformed. This meant abandoning the system of central control and planning that had been in operation since Stalin.

Glasnost means 'openness' — all the peoples of the USSR were to be given greater freedom. The power of the secret police (the KGB) was reduced and free elections were held in 1990.

The Soviet Union under Gorbachev

By 1985 the Soviet Union was bankrupt and Gorbachev knew that survival meant seeking financial and technological aid from the West. Industry was hopelessly inefficient, with 40% of factories working at a loss. It was estimated that 25% of economic activity was on the black market.

Gorbachev sought to maintain the power of the Communist Party but, following the changes he introduced, the people of the Soviet-dominated world wanted to be rid of it. He hoped to introduce change through two key ideas: *perestroika* and *glasnost*.

These changes came too late. Gorbachev did not receive the financial aid that he had expected from the USA and by the late-1980s many ethnic groups were demanding independence from the USSR. Gorbachev withdrew troops from the Baltic States. This was the signal for the collapse of the Soviet empire.

Inadvertently, glasnost and perestroika had helped to bring down Communism. By 1992 the Soviet Union had ceased to exist.

The USA
1918–80

The 1920s and the Wall Street Crash

After the First World War the USA followed a policy of isolation and kept involvement with the world to a minimum.

◆ The economy of the USA grew strongly during the First World War and took many markets from its European competitors. Agriculture also prospered during the war years and many people expected things to remain unchanged in the 1920s.

◆ The postwar presidents (Harding, Coolidge and Hoover) all believed in the policy of 'laissez-faire', i.e. that the federal government should not interfere in the economy.

◆ In 1922 Congress passed the Fordney–McCumber tariff, which put high duties on many imports to the USA.

The boom

The 1920s saw a consumer boom in the USA. Ordinary people were able to buy cars, electrical goods and household gadgets because of the development of mass production. Henry Ford pioneered the idea of making goods on an assembly line. The average price of a car went down from $850 in 1908 to $250 in 1925.

If anyone was unable to buy any of these mass-produced goods, there were ways to help purchasers. Hire purchase became a way of life. However, not all groups prospered in the boom of the 1920s. Farmers were the first to experience problems, as European agriculture began to recover.

Farmers who grew barley or grapes were worst hit, when **Prohibition** was introduced. Many farmers tried to compensate for this by producing as much food as possible but, as a result, prices fell and their problems worsened.

Causes and consequences of the Wall Street Crash

The boom led to over-production and in some industries, such as car manufacture, skilled workers lost their jobs. In addition, exports began to dry up as other countries put up tariff barriers in response to the Fordney–McCumber Act.

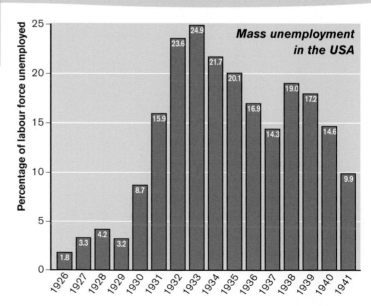

Mass unemployment in the USA

(Percentage of labour force unemployed)

1926: 1.8
1927: 3.3
1928: 4.2
1929: 3.2
1930: 8.7
1931: 15.9
1932: 23.6
1933: 24.9
1934: 21.7
1935: 20.1
1936: 16.9
1937: 14.3
1938: 19.0
1939: 17.2
1940: 14.6
1941: 9.9

Speculation on the stock market

Those companies which prospered enjoyed steady increases in the value of their shares. In response to this, people began to buy shares on a large scale in the hope of making easy money. There were almost no controls on the buying and selling of shares and the USA seemed to be in the grip of a share-buying frenzy.

The collapse in share prices

The Crash of 24 October 1929 saw the most calamitous fall in share prices the world had seen. But the collapse was not confined to one day; it led to a shattering of confidence in the financial system, and the Depression of the 1930s. Between September 1929 and July 1932 the value of shares on Wall Street fell from $89.6 billion to $15.6 billion. The table below shows what happened to the shares of some leading American companies.

| | Price per share (US $) | |
	1929	1932
US Steel	262	22
General Motors	73	8
Montgomery Ward	138	4
American Telephone & Telegraph Co. (AT&T)	304	72

'On the margin'

Spotting the share bonanza, some people borrowed money to buy shares. Others bought 'on the margin' — that is, they paid only 10% of the share value to acquire the shares, expecting to pay the full price once the shares had risen in value. This was fine, provided that confidence in the US economy remained high.

Some investors realised that the boom could not last and began to sell shares to cash in on their gains. A trickle became a flood and in October this led to the Wall Street Crash.

Effects of the Crash

- Many people were bankrupted.
- Farmers with mortgages had to surrender their farms.
- Savings in banks were lost.
- Homeowners lost their homes.
- 10,000 banks stopped trading.
- Demand for goods fell.
- Unemployment rose.

Exam watch

Learn the concepts — investment, 'on the margin', overproduction. Ensure you can explain why the Depression came.

Government reaction to the Crash

President Hoover believed that government should not interfere in business and did nothing to help those affected by the Crash. However, confidence was severely shaken and the US economy went into recession. Unemployment rose rapidly to 17 million. The recession spread to Europe and caused the worldwide **Depression** of the 1930s.

Eventually, Hoover did take some action. He reduced taxes and passed the Hawley–Smoot Tariff to protect US industry. In 1932 he set up the Reconstruction Finance Corporation, which lent money to banks, industry and agriculture.

Roosevelt's New Deal

President Hoover continued to believe in the idea of 'rugged individualism'. He did not accept that the federal government should try to engineer a recovery and he became ever more unpopular. In the 1932 presidential election, the Democratic candidate was Franklin Delano Roosevelt, who campaigned and won on the basis of offering the people of the USA a **New Deal**.

Legislation for the New Deal

Roosevelt knew he had to be pro-active and his first one hundred days as president saw him pass a mass of laws to try to take the USA out of the Depression:

The **Emergency Banking Relief Act** closed all banks for four days to quieten things down. Government officials investigated them and they could only re-open if they had sufficient reserve funds. Banks were banned from investing in the stock market. This restored confidence in the banks.

The **Agricultural Adjustment Act** encouraged farmers to switch to new crops and paid them to stop over-producing others. Farm incomes rose again. Farmers had to reduce the amount of land under the plough and kill many animals. This measure was widely criticised for wasting food at a time when millions were starving.

The **Tennessee Valley Authority** built a whole series of dams to control the flood waters of the Tennessee River. This meant that the land could be irrigated and farmed and it also provided electricity. Industries such as aluminium smelting and paper-making were attracted to the area. Many jobs were created in a poor and backward area of the USA.

The **Federal Emergency Relief Agency** provided $500 million for immediate relief of the poorest victims of the Depression.

The **Civilian Conservation Corps** provided work for 2,000,000 young Americans (only 8,000 women) in the countryside, clearing forests, replanting trees, mending fences etc. Young people worked for 6 months to get used to work. They were paid, but had to send most of their earnings home. Although many young people took part, they often moved from one camp to another and rarely found permanent work.

The **National Recovery Administration** supervised major building schemes, which provided jobs, and also implemented agreements between employers and workers to establish decent wages and working conditions.

The Second New Deal

The original New Deal programme covered the years 1933–35. In 1935 the Second New Deal was heralded with measures which extended the benefits conferred on the poor and the unemployed to all sections of society, chiefly:

◆ The **Wagner Act** gave all workers the right to join a trade union.
◆ The **Works Progress Administration** provided government money for many improvement schemes all over the USA: bridges, hospitals, schools, airports, parks. Even writers and artists were hired to write local guides and paint murals.
◆ The **Social Security Act** set up a basic system of welfare, including old age pensions, and unemployment and sick pay.

Opposition to the New Deal

- ◆ **Republicans** complained about Roosevelt spending too much money. They said the New Deal was tackling unemployment only by turning millions of people into government employees. They also complained that the New Deal gave the federal government too much power.
- ◆ **Big business** attacked Roosevelt because he was giving too much power to the trade unions. The Supreme Court backed these views, declaring in 1935 that the National Recovery Administration was illegal. The Agricultural Adjustment Act was also condemned in 1936.
- ◆ In 1937 Roosevelt tried to increase the size of the **Supreme Court** from 9 to 15 judges — by appointing six new ones more sympathetic to his policies. He was forced to back down by public opinion. It was thought that he was becoming too powerful; some even said he was acting like a dictator.
- ◆ Some believed that there was a different way to reconcile rich and poor. In 1935 Senator Huey Long of Louisiana started the 'Share our Wealth' campaign, planning to tax the rich to give every family a basic income of $5,000. He intended to stand against Roosevelt in the 1936 presidential election, but was murdered earlier in the year.

Watts Bar Dam construction on the Tennessee River

 Exam watch

Focus on why there was opposition from various groups. Ensure you can make a judgement about the success/failure of Roosevelt.

Look for continuity. How did things move on?

An overall assessment

There is much debate about how effective the New Deal really was. It was only partially successful.

Successes

By 1940 unemployment in America had fallen by about 40% since 1933.

Roosevelt gave people hope and restored their confidence in the government and the financial system. His 'fireside chats', and the replies people received to their letters to the White House, convinced many Americans that the USA would pull through.

Black Americans were given access to the Civilian Conservation Corps, although they had separate camps. Black leaders voted strongly for Roosevelt as a result.

The huge programmes of building roads, bridges, harbours and so on created a more efficient infrastructure.

Failures

Recovery was only partial. In 1937 industry was still only working at 75% of its 1929 level and unemployment rose that year when government intervention was reduced.

Many of the schemes that Roosevelt started lasted only a few months. The schemes run by the Civilian Conservation Corps gave only temporary relief.

US trade with the rest of the world did not recover.

Black Americans saw little improvement in their civil rights. Roosevelt needed the votes of (anti-Black) southern Democrats to get his laws through. New Deal laws still allowed black Americans to be paid less than Whites.

Women made little progress towards equality and they too were still paid less than men for the same work.

The USA and the Second World War

The Japanese attack on Pearl Harbor, 1941

How did the war affect the lives of US citizens?

◆ Unemployment fell rapidly. In early 1941 there were still 8 million people out of work, despite the New Deal; by the end of 1942 unemployment had fallen dramatically.

◆ 16 million US citizens served in the armed forces and a good proportion were sent to Europe. Many had never left the USA before.

◆ The number of working mothers increased dramatically, leading to a rise in juvenile crime. The proportion of women working rose from 27% to 37% between 1941 and 1945.

◆ There was strong government pressure on women to work. However, at the end of the war, many women were persuaded to give up work and return to family life.

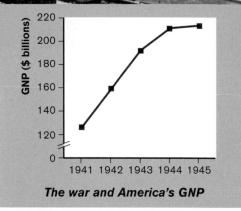

The war and America's GNP

Note: GNP (gross national product) is a measure of how much a country produces in a year.

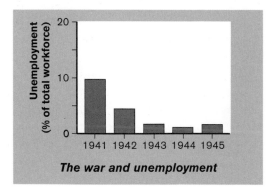

The war and unemployment

The impact of the war on black people

The sense of common purpose fostered by the war, and the necessity to harness all available manpower, gave black people the opportunity for advancement.

◆ About 1 million black Americans served in the armed forces, though they served in separate units. Black officers were also appointed in all three services. The air force began to train black pilots, 600 of whom had completed their training by the end of the war.

◆ Roosevelt attempted to force industry to employ Blacks. In 1941 he set up the Fair Employment Practices Committee, but it had no power to enforce his policy, except to refuse to give government contracts to companies that would not cooperate.

◆ 700,000 black Americans moved north and west from the southern states, and were able to find jobs which not only paid more but offered a chance to acquire skills.

◆ Membership of the National Association for the Advancement of Colored People (NAACP) grew during the war and by 1945 had 460,000 members.

Japanese Americans

When war broke out it was decided to move 110,000 Japanese Americans from their homes on the West Coast, because they might be a security risk. Even those Japanese born in the USA were removed. Many were forced to sell their belongings and were moved to internment camps where conditions were very poor.

Exam watch

Ensure you know about the impact of the war on different groups — women, black Americans, Japanese Americans.

After the war

The USA had always been suspicious of Communism, and its encroaching influence in Europe after 1945 led the USA to formulate a policy of opposing Soviet domination. President Truman, who succeeded Roosevelt in 1945, was particularly concerned with 'containing Communism'.

◆ In 1947 the USA announced the **Truman Doctrine** and the **Marshall Plan**. These were designed to help countries in Europe militarily and economically, and the intention was to halt the spread of Communism.

◆ Truman talked also of a Communist threat inside the US and approved the Federal Employee Loyalty Program, which involved every federal worker being investigated for Communist sympathies. Four million people were checked and no cases of spying were discovered. This was the start of the **Red Scare**, which led to **McCarthyism**.

McCarthyism

Senator Joe McCarthy

Fear of Communism grew after 1945. Soviet expansion in Eastern Europe, the Communist takeover in China, the Russian explosion of an atomic bomb in 1949 and the Korean War which began in 1950 all showed the danger.

Many Americans also believed that Communism was a real threat to the USA. In 1950 Senator Joe McCarthy claimed to have a list of many known Communists working for the US government; but he also accused scientists, diplomats, actors, film producers and writers of being sympathisers. People were anxious and frightened by the growing threat and were inclined to believe McCarthy's extravagant claims. The 'witch hunt' built to fever pitch.

- Few cases were ever brought, but the one against Alger Hiss in 1948 added fuel to McCarthy's accusations. Hiss was sentenced to five years in jail in 1950 but always protested his innocence.
- After the Hiss trial the McCarran Internal Security Act was passed, which stated that it was illegal for Americans to take part in any actions that might bring about a Communist government in the USA.
- Immediately after the Hiss case, the Rosenbergs were arrested for spying for the Soviet Union and were eventually executed.
- McCarthy claimed that he had a list of 205 Communists working in the State Department.

Alger Hiss takes the stand after being accused of membership of a Communist spy ring, August 1948

- Many Americans believed that McCarthy was defending the country; they saw him as a crusader against Communism.
- McCarthy was clever in the way he presented his cases. He was always on the attack; if anybody stood up to him, he accused them as well. Few people were prepared to stand up to him, not even President Truman.
- As chairman of the House Un-American Activities Committee in the US Senate, McCarthy exercised real power in Washington and had ready access to television and the media.
- In 1953 President Eisenhower agreed to an investigation of the civil service and nearly 7,000 people lost their jobs. Even General Marshall had to resign for supposedly 'deliberately allowing Communist victories'.
- McCarthy was a skilful and powerful speaker and he created such an atmosphere of hysteria that no one knew what to believe.

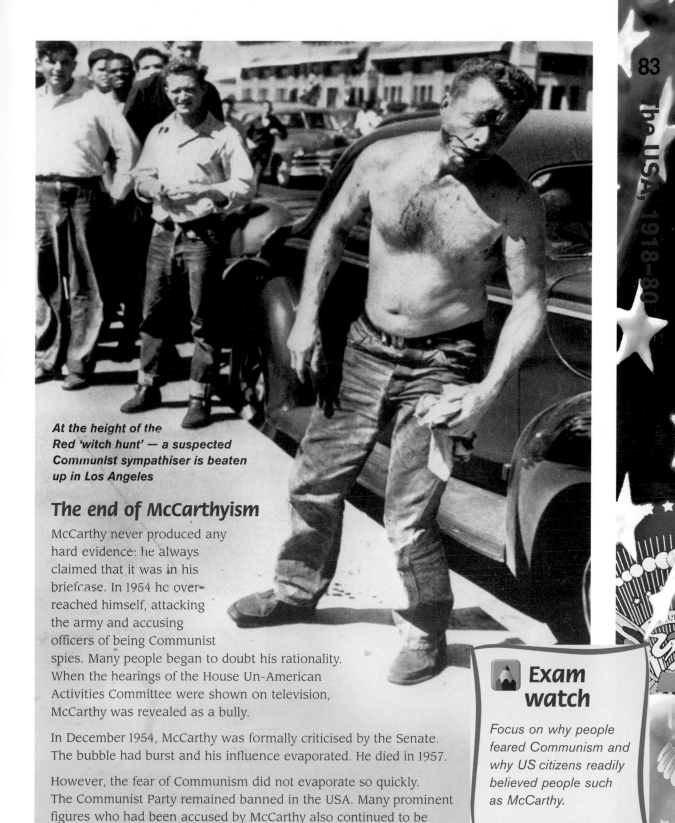

At the height of the Red 'witch hunt' — a suspected Communist sympathiser is beaten up in Los Angeles

The end of McCarthyism

McCarthy never produced any hard evidence: he always claimed that it was in his briefcase. In 1954 he over-reached himself, attacking the army and accusing officers of being Communist spies. Many people began to doubt his rationality. When the hearings of the House Un-American Activities Committee were shown on television, McCarthy was revealed as a bully.

In December 1954, McCarthy was formally criticised by the Senate. The bubble had burst and his influence evaporated. He died in 1957.

However, the fear of Communism did not evaporate so quickly. The Communist Party remained banned in the USA. Many prominent figures who had been accused by McCarthy also continued to be blacklisted and refused offers of work for years to come.

> **📷 Exam watch**
>
> *Focus on why people feared Communism and why US citizens readily believed people such as McCarthy.*

Campaign for civil rights

Black Americans did not have the same rights as Whites. In the southern states, whose economies had originally depended on slavery, they had their own separate facilities. The 'Jim Crow Laws' were supposed to ensure that black Americans had separate but equal facilities — but they were never as good. Blacks were treated as second-class citizens.

The National Association for the Advancement of Colored People (NAACP) had been founded in 1909 to raise the issue of their denial of civil rights. The experiences of black Americans during the war encouraged hopes that there would be real changes when the war ended.

The development of the civil rights movement

President Truman ended segregation in units of the armed forces after the Second World War. But education became the key area for changes to civil rights. In 1950 the Supreme Court declared that black and white students could not be segregated in the same school, and that the education provided in segregated schools had to be equal in every respect. Two key cases tested the even-handedness implied by this ruling.

Brown v Topeka
In 1954 Oliver Brown used the Supreme Court ruling to take the City of Topeka in Kansas to court for not allowing his daughter to attend a nearby Whites-only school. She was forced to attend one some distance away. The NAACP supported the case, which Brown won.

Little Rock, Arkansas
Immediately after the Brown case there was another. Elizabeth Eckford and eight other black students tried to enrol at Little Rock High School in Arkansas. She was stopped by the State Governor who surrounded the school with the state National Guard. President Eisenhower sent troops to escort and protect her and the other students. The troops remained at the school for a year.

The Supreme Court declared all segregated schools to be illegal.

White students shout insults at Elizabeth Eckford outside Little Rock High School, Arkansas

Civil disobedience

In 1955 Rosa Parks was arrested in Montgomery, Alabama, for refusing to give up her seat on a bus to a white man. **Martin Luther King** organised a boycott of the buses, which lasted for a year until the bus company gave in. In 1956 the Supreme Court ruled that segregation on buses was illegal.

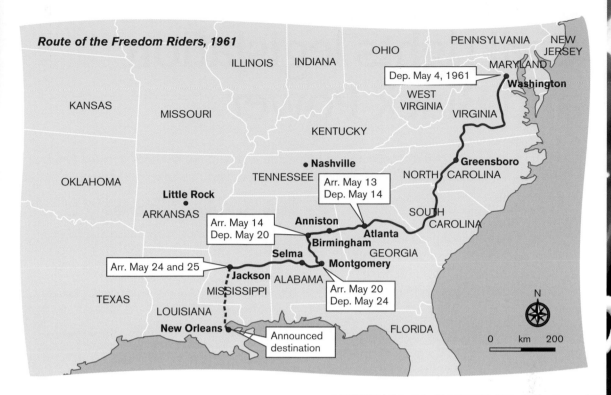

Route of the Freedom Riders, 1961

Dep. May 4, 1961 — Washington

Arr. May 13
Dep. May 14

Arr. May 14
Dep. May 20

Arr. May 24 and 25

Arr. May 20
Dep. May 24

Announced destination

The campaign gathers momentum

◆ President Kennedy had relied on the black vote to secure his election and he was determined to bring about equality for Blacks. He began to appoint black Americans to important positions.

◆ In 1961 civil rights campaigners, the Freedom Riders, began to make bus journeys to break the Jim Crow Laws. They were arrested, but gained tremendous publicity. All railway and bus stations were subsequently desegregated.

◆ In 1962 Kennedy sent troops to Mississippi University to protect James Meredith, a black student, and defend his right to study there.

◆ Also in 1962 the city of Birmingham, Alabama, closed all public parks to avoid integrating them. Martin Luther King organised a campaign of disobedience and protesters were attacked with water cannon, dogs and baton charges. Arrests reached 500 a day, but it was all shown on television and most people were sickened by the violence used by the authorities in breaking up the demonstrations.

Martin Luther King was founder of the Southern Christian Leadership Conference. He began to organise non-violent protests all over the South. The main method of protest was the sit-in, and images of peaceful Blacks being removed by National Guardsmen were seen across the nation.

 Exam watch

Focus on key cases and *the notion of the support of the presidents and the Supreme Court.*

Civil rights legislation and Black Power

Rather than cope with civil disobedience and the strife it generated, Kennedy decided to introduce a civil rights bill to Congress. He wanted the nation to back his actions. But he was not prepared to force the measure through and possibly lose the support of Congress.

When Martin Luther King planned a march through Washington in support of the bill, Kennedy asked him to call it off. King refused and 200,000 people marched.

Things changed after Kennedy's assassination in 1963. There was a great wave of sympathy for him and for his aims. An important **Civil Rights Act** was passed in 1964.

The Civil Rights Act, 1964

- Made segregation in education and housing illegal
- Stated that all Americans were entitled to equal employment opportunities
- Stated that all federal projects must include racial integration

The **Voting Rights Act, 1965** made it illegal to try to prevent Blacks from registering for the vote by setting literacy tests for voters.

The Black Power movement

For some young black Americans, the pace of change was too slow. They were not prepared to wait for King's peaceful tactics to win them equality.

There was growing interest in Islam, which was seen as a black religion, and growing intolerance of what young Blacks saw as continuing white supremacy. A number of different leaders were emerging:

- **Malcolm X** was a leader of the Black Muslims and founder of the Nation of Islam. He advocated violence as a means of self-defence for Blacks who were oppressed by Whites.

Malcolm X

- **Stokeley Carmichael** wanted to establish a completely separate black society in America.
- **The Black Panthers** wanted to start a race war against white Americans.

The Black Panthers

- Riots broke out in many US cities. In 1965 there were serious riots in the Watts area of Los Angeles and 34 people died. There were further riots in the next three years in Chicago, Philadelphia, Cleveland and New York. 1967 was the worst year, with 150 cities affected. It seemed that civil war was breaking out in the USA.
- In 1968 Martin Luther King was assassinated by an extremist and his death sparked off a new wave of riots.

Civil rights march in Jackson, Mississippi, 1966

The Civil Rights Act, 1968

- Banned discrimination in housing
- Made it an offence to injure civil rights workers
- Made it an offence even to cross a state boundary with intent to harm civil rights activists

Civil rights became less of an issue by the late-1960s, because some of the reforms of President Johnson were seen to have had a positive effect. But it was also overshadowed by the war in Vietnam, which had emerged as the most important issue for protest in the USA.

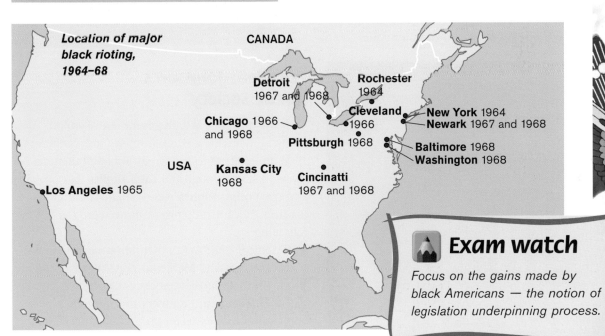

Location of major black rioting, 1964–68

CANADA

Detroit 1967 and 1968

Rochester 1964

Cleveland 1966

New York 1964
Newark 1967 and 1968

Chicago 1966 and 1968

Pittsburgh 1968

Baltimore 1968
Washington 1968

USA

Kansas City 1968

Cincinatti 1967 and 1968

Los Angeles 1965

Exam watch

Focus on the gains made by black Americans — the notion of legislation underpinning process.

New concepts for a new society

President Kennedy's 'New Frontier'

The New Frontier was John Kennedy's idea of a programme to get the USA going again. He believed that the country had stagnated under Eisenhower. Kennedy wanted to appeal to the younger generation.

John Kennedy

The New Frontier included:
◆ attempts to increase economic growth and reduce unemployment
◆ a $900 million programme of public works
◆ a general tax cut and an increase in the minimum wage from $1.00 to $1.25
◆ an Area Redevelopment Act, which allowed the federal government to give loans and grants to states which had problems with long-term unemployment
◆ a Manpower and Training Act that provided retraining for the unemployed
◆ a Housing Act that provided cheap loans for the redevelopment of inner cities

How successful was the New Frontier?

The measures introduced were all very successful, although the real effects were felt only after Kennedy's death. Less successful were:
◆ Medicare, a system of state health insurance
◆ attempts to improve education and housing

Lyndon Johnson

President Johnson's 'Great Society'

This was the renewal programme of Lyndon Johnson, who succeeded Kennedy in November 1963. In addition to the Great Society initiative, Johnson saw through the **Civil Rights Act** of 1964 and the **Voting Rights Act** of 1965. The main features of Johnson's programme were the following:
◆ a Medical Care Act, which improved Medicare (for the old) and Medicaid (for the poor) and sought to ensure equal access to health for all
◆ the Appalachian Recovery programme, which provided money to an area with economic and social problems

- setting up the Office of Economic Opportunity, to help poor people in inner cities with education, loans and community projects. This was the basis of Johnson's Programme for Poverty
- the Elementary and Secondary Education Act, which provided the first major federal support for state education

 Exam watch

Look at the two-pronged approach — civil rights advances and aid to weaker sections of society.

How successful was the Great Society?

At the beginning of his presidency, Johnson took advantage of the sympathy for the government after the death of Kennedy. He wanted to use government funds to eliminate poverty, which he saw as a blight on the richest society in the world. He was only partially successful:

- There was opposition from both Democrats and Republicans to the scale of this 'social engineering'.
- Johnson also had to reduce the scale of some of the projects because of the cost of the Vietnam War.

The 1960s: liberation and protest

The changing role of women

Just as in Europe, the Second World War gave women new opportunities. They had proved themselves in the workplace and in the war effort, and many women wanted more prominent roles than simply as housewives and mothers.

Rising affluence also gave women greater freedom to assert their independence. The birth control pill became available in the 1960s, reducing the dependency of relationships. In 1961 Kennedy appointed Eleanor Roosevelt to lead a Commission on the Status of Women, which caught the prevailing mood. Other advances followed:

- The Equal Pay Act of 1963 stated that men and women had to be given the same pay for the same job.
- Betty Friedan's influential book *The Feminine Mystique*, demanding equal rights for women, was published in 1963.
- As well as heralding important advances for Blacks, the Civil Rights Act of 1964 banned discrimination on the basis of gender.

Betty Friedan, founder and first president of the National Organisation for Women

Occupational group	1950	1960	1970	1980
All workers	28	33	38	44
White-collar	40	43	48	55
Professional	40	38	40	46
Managerial	14	14	17	28
Clerical	62	68	74	81
Sales	34	37	39	49
Blue-collar	24	26	30	34
Crafts	3	3	5	6
Operatives	27	28	32	34
Labourers	4	4	8	11
Private household	95	96	96	97
Other services	45	52	55	61
Farm workers	9	10	10	17

The percentage of women working in various occupations, 1950–80

◆ In 1966 the National Organisation for Women was set up and in 1972 the Educational Amendment Act out-lawed sex discrimination in education.

Exam watch

Focus on why there were protests — especially from different sections of society.

The student movement

Young Americans were the most affluent in the world and in the 1950s they had money to spend as never before. A youth culture, with a separate identity, started to emerge, fuelled by popular music. Rock and roll music was new, lively, optimistic — and young. The younger generation of the 1950s had their own idols, such as the singer Elvis Presley and the actor James Dean.

Young people felt more confident and independent. At the same time, more of them were going to 'college'. New universities and community colleges sprang up all over America to satisfy the desire for tertiary education. An affluent and independent 'student generation' was born — and it soon found its voice:

Bob Dylan — protest singer

◆ Protest singers such as Bob Dylan and Joan Baez gained enormous popularity. In their songs they attacked govern-ment corruption, war and racism.
◆ In 1964 Students for a Democratic Society was formed. Its chief purpose was to attack the role of the US in the Vietnam War. By the end of 1965 it had 10,000 members at 150 colleges and universities across the USA.
◆ The bombing of North Vietnam in 1965 led to a rash of student protests. Students felt themselves to be uncomfortably close to this vicious war against a hapless enemy. Three million Americans served in the war and their average age was 19. Many resorted to drugs to help them cope with the horrors of the war.
◆ The protests reached a peak in 1968, when the 'peaceniks' brandishing only 'flower power' exhorted everyone to 'make love, not war'.

Watergate

Nixon seeks re-election

The scandal unfolds

The Watergate scandal was caused by an attempt to 'bug' the offices of the Democratic Party in the Watergate building in Washington. Five men were found to have broken into the building in June 1972 and were arrested. The men were employed by the Committee to Re-elect the President (CREEP). The President seeking re-election was the Republican, Richard Nixon.

At first, the break-in was a minor news story. However, due to the relentless investigation of two journalists, Bernstein and Woodward, the unfolding drama gripped America:

1 President Nixon stated that the White House was not involved in any of these activities, but at the same time he authorised the payment of $460,000 to the five men.

2 The trial of the arrested men took place after Nixon was re-elected in 1972. One of them admitted in court that the White House had been involved.

3 A Senate Committee was set up to investigate and as the involvement of Nixon's close aides became apparent, many of them were forced to resign. The President, however, continued to deny any prior knowledge of the plan. He even appointed a special investigator. He said, 'There will be no whitewash at the White House.'

4 It was then revealed that all conversations in the White House since 1971 had been recorded on tape. The Senate demanded to hear the tapes, but Nixon refused to hand them over.

5 Some tapes were eventually handed over in November 1973. When they were revealed, the public was shocked by Nixon's foul and obscene language. But the tapes had been edited.

6 Nixon finally handed over the unedited tapes, but only after a ruling from the Supreme Court and an announcement by the House of Representatives that it was about to begin impeachment proceedings.

7 The tapes proved that Nixon had lied and that he had tried to prevent the investigation, but not that he had known about the original break-in and bugging. He resigned in August 1974 to avoid the disgrace of impeachment.

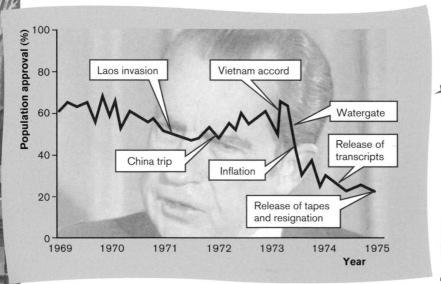

*Inside one of the offices of the **Washington Post**, Carl Bernstein and Bob Woodward discuss developments in their explosive story, April 1973*

Effects of the scandal

Thirty-one of Nixon's advisers went to prison as a result of the investigation. The American people were shocked and dismayed by Nixon's shabby actions, his continual evasions and deceit. They felt that their trust had been betrayed and, following the scandal, Congress passed laws to limit the power of the President:

◆ Congress had to be consulted before US troops were sent into action.
◆ Federal money could not be used for personal purposes.
◆ The Election Campaign Act set limits on contributions to presidential campaign funds.
◆ The Privacy Act allowed citizens access to files kept on them by the government.

Gallup poll of Nixon's popularity

Population approval (%)

- Laos invasion
- Vietnam accord
- China trip
- Inflation
- Watergate
- Release of transcripts
- Release of tapes and resignation

Year: 1969 1970 1971 1972 1973 1974 1975

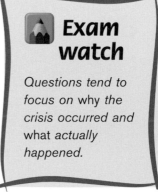

Exam watch

Questions tend to focus on why the crisis occurred and what actually happened.

The Cold War
1945–90

Beginnings of the Cold War

Why did the USA and USSR become rivals, 1945–49?

American and Soviet forces met in 1945 to celebrate the end of Nazi Germany. They seemed friendly enough — but for how long? Disagreements between the USA, the Soviet Union and Britain broke out even before the war had ended. Why?
◆ They had been uneasy allies.
◆ They had different ideologies.

> **The Communists (USSR)** espoused state ownership of factories, land, farms and transport, a one-party dictatorship and no free elections. The Comintern tried to spread world Communist revolution.

> **The capitalists (USA)** believed in the private ownership of businesses run for profit, democratic free elections and more than one political party so that power could change hands.

Before the Second World War had even started, there was a history of mistrust between Communist Russia and the capitalist states, such as the USA, Britain and France:
◆ The Western powers had tried to destroy the Communists by invading Russia (1918–21).
◆ Stalin, the Soviet leader, thought that Britain and France were encouraging Hitler to attack the Communists.
◆ Britain and France were both shocked by the Nazi–Soviet Pact (see page 30).
◆ During the war, Stalin complained that the USA and Britain were slow to invade Europe to take the pressure off the Soviet Union, which was fighting a better war against Hitler.

The immediate causes of the Cold War

◆ As the Second World War drew to a close, cracks began appearing in the Grand Alliance against Hitler. The Red Army of 6 million soldiers was flooding into Germany and Eastern Europe.
◆ The Allies met twice to try to shape the future peace:

  1 Yalta (in the USSR)
    Date: February 1945
    Present: Churchill, Roosevelt and Stalin

  2 Potsdam (in Germany)
    Date: July 1945
    Present: Stalin, Truman and Attlee

Decisions made at Yalta and Potsdam

Germany was divided into four zones of military occupation.

Berlin (in the Soviet zone) was also divided into four sectors of military occupation.

Germany was to pay reparations. Stalin wanted $20 billion, although the Americans disagreed with such a harsh figure.

'Free' elections would take place, so that the people of Eastern Europe could choose their own governments.

Germany would be run by a joint Allied Control Commission.

Germany would be 'deNazified' and war criminals put on trial at Nuremberg.

A United Nations Organisation was to be set up.

Were the Allies in dispute?

Certainly there were suspicions and mistrust.

The United States was angry that 22 million people in Eastern Europe had come under Soviet control. Would they try to dominate Western Europe too? Stalin also would not allow the people of Eastern Europe to choose their own governments; Communist ones were imposed in Poland, Czechoslovakia, Hungary, Romania and Bulgaria.

The USSR had every intention of safeguarding itself from future invasions by installing friendly governments on its borders. Stalin was also suspicious of the USA for keeping its atomic bomb a secret from him.

Britain, too, was concerned about the advancing tide of Soviet Communism. Although no longer in power, Winston Churchill had made a speech in Fulton (USA) in 1946. He complained that an 'Iron Curtain' had descended across Europe. Britain was struggling to help the King of Greece to fight Communist guerrillas for control of the country. Britain told the USA in 1947 that it could not continue with this help. Turkey was also under threat from Communists. What would the USA do?

The Truman Doctrine

In a speech made in March 1947, President Truman of the USA proclaimed the 'Truman Doctrine'. He said that the USA would oppose Communist expansion all over the world. 'I believe that it must be the policy of the United States to support free peoples, who are resisting attempted subjugation by armed minorities or by outside pressure,' Truman announced. $400 million was given to Turkey and Greece — and the Communist threats there were defeated. How would the Truman Doctrine help the rest of Europe, though? This came in the form of Marshall Aid (see overleaf).

Containment in Europe, 1947–49

Why was there conflict over Berlin? Three key concepts explain it:

Containment

The USA had committed itself to containing the Soviet threat. The aim was to stop the further expansion of Communism anywhere on the globe.

The Marshall Plan

Europe was weak. There were famine, refugees, low production, disease and, in 1947, a harsh winter. This was a perfect breeding ground for Communism, or so the Americans thought. The plan put forward by the US Secretary of State, George Marshall, was to spend billions of dollars on European recovery, so that Europe could — and would — defend itself against Communism.

The Soviet view of the Marshall Plan

The USSR argued that the USA was using economic imperialism to bribe countries to unite against the Soviet Union and threaten its safety. The plan, according to Stalin, was for President Truman to bring more states under US influence and build up their military power. So, in 1947, Cominform (Communist Information Bureau) was set up to help the Communist parties of Europe work together.

The Marshall Plan: key elements

◆ In 1948–52 $13 billion was given to 16 European states; most of it went to Britain and France.
◆ The money was spent on food, animal feed, fertiliser, housing, and to help produce machinery.
◆ The USA also offered funds to Communist satellite states, but Stalin prevented Marshall Aid from reaching the East.
◆ US aid helped to prevent the spread of Communism.

The Berlin Airlift Crisis, 1948–49

Decisions made at Yalta and Potsdam had left Berlin in a vulnerable position. It lay deep inside the Soviet zone, but was also divided between the four winning countries. Britain, France and the USA relied on the Soviet Union to allow access across their zone by rail and road to their sectors of Berlin. In 1946 the three Western sectors formed an economic union. As Marshall Aid poured into West Berlin, Stalin warned that he regarded this as a threat, especially if it encouraged the growth of a strong Germany.

Key
France
Great Britain
United States
Soviet Union
— Air corridor

Occupied Germany from 1945

A dangerous chain of events

1948:

1 Britain and the USA introduced a new currency into the zones of Germany controlled by the West, to help economic recovery. Stalin was kept in the dark about this.

2 Stalin continued to strip the Russian zone of reparations, to ensure that Germany was ruined.

3 In March Soviet troops began to interfere with traffic going to West Berlin.

4 On 24 June all land routes to West Berlin were cut by the Soviet Union. Stalin clearly intended to force the Western Allies to leave Berlin.

5 How would West Berlin be supplied? By an airlift — 4,000 tons of food, fuel, clothing and medicines would need to be flown in through narrow air corridors.

6 During the winter, the Soviets cut off electricity supplies.

1949:

7 In April a record 1,400 planes landed in West Berlin.

8 In May, after secret talks, the blockade was brought to an end.

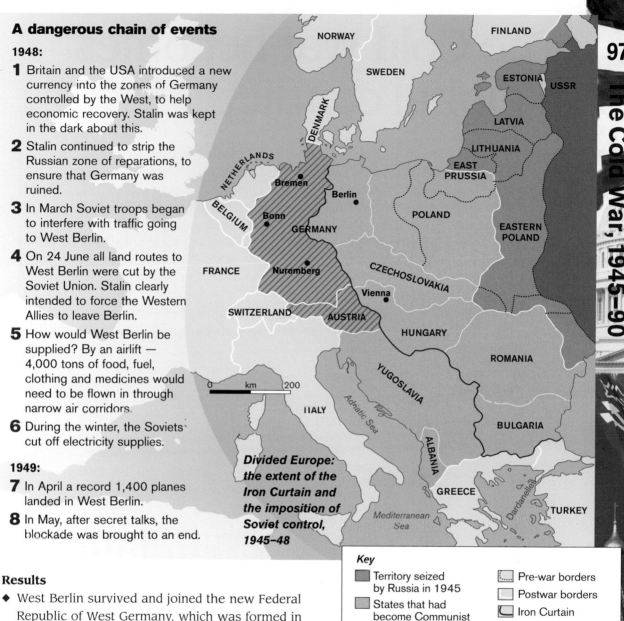

Divided Europe: the extent of the Iron Curtain and the imposition of Soviet control, 1945–48

Key

▨ Territory seized by Russia in 1945	⬚ Pre-war borders
▨ States that had become Communist by 1949	▢ Postwar borders
	▢ Iron Curtain
	▨ Allied zones

Results

◆ West Berlin survived and joined the new Federal Republic of West Germany, which was formed in May 1949 through the amalgamation of the British, French and US zones.

◆ On the other side of the 'Iron Curtain', the German Democratic Republic was formed in October 1949.

◆ Both Germany and Berlin remained divided until 1990.

◆ NATO (the North Atlantic Treaty Organisation) was formed by 12 Western countries in response to the Soviet threat.

◆ Mutual suspicion between West and East deepened. Watch towers and concrete defences faced each other across Europe and the Cold War intensified.

 Exam watch

Why did the USA and USSR become rivals in the period 1945–49? Which side bears more of the blame — the USA or the USSR? Why was Berlin such an important cause of worsening relations between the USA and the USSR?

The Cold War becomes a global conflict

American concerns about the spread of Communism outside Europe continued to increase.

◆ In 1949 a Communist government took control of China.

◆ Also in 1949 the USSR caught up with American nuclear technology and exploded its own atomic bomb. The arms race was set to escalate, as both powers began to develop hydrogen bombs — which were many times more destructive.

◆ President Truman feared that Communism was spreading according to the 'domino theory'. This theory suggested that once one country in Asia fell to Communism, then its neighbour would soon follow — and so on. There was concern that this might apply to Malaya, Indonesia, Burma, Cambodia and Vietnam.

◆ In the USA Senator Joseph McCarthy was carrying out a witchhunt into 'Un-American Activities'. His Senate Committee attempted to root out Communists in both the US government and society.

Alliance systems

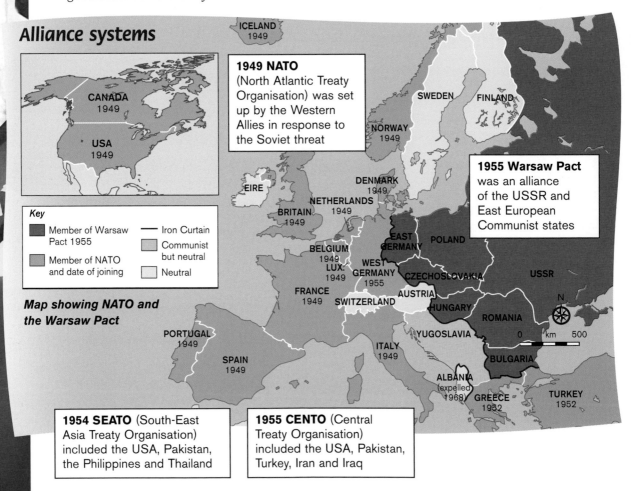

1949 NATO (North Atlantic Treaty Organisation) was set up by the Western Allies in response to the Soviet threat

1955 Warsaw Pact was an alliance of the USSR and East European Communist states

Key
- Member of Warsaw Pact 1955
- Member of NATO and date of joining
- Iron Curtain
- Communist but neutral
- Neutral

Map showing NATO and the Warsaw Pact

1954 SEATO (South-East Asia Treaty Organisation) included the USA, Pakistan, the Philippines and Thailand

1955 CENTO (Central Treaty Organisation) included the USA, Pakistan, Turkey, Iran and Iraq

War in Korea, 1950–53

Korea had been in Japanese hands since 1910. In 1945 Soviet troops defeated the Japanese in the northern part of Korea, while US troops freed the south. Korea was divided along the 38th Parallel and it proved impossible to unite the two halves of the country. In 1948 US and Soviet troops left Korea. North Korea was ruled by a Communist dictatorship under Kim Il Sung. The south was ruled by another dictator, Syngman Rhee, who was a capitalist. Hatred between the north and south became bitter.

Stage 1

June to September 1950

June 1950
North Korean forces, probably encouraged by Stalin, invaded the south, captured its capital Seoul and overran all of the country except for a small area round Pusan.

July 1950
American troops were sent to help South Korea. The United Nations Security Council met in the absence of the USSR. Communist China had no seat on the Security Council, so there was no Communist veto to prevent the UN taking action.

Stage 2

The UN decided to send troops to assist South Korea. In September 1950, under their commander General MacArthur, UN troops landed at Inchon. More UN troops broke out from Pusan and the Communist forces were pushed back. Seoul was recaptured and UN troops advanced quickly. These troops were made up of soldiers from 18 countries, but came primarily from the USA and South Korea.

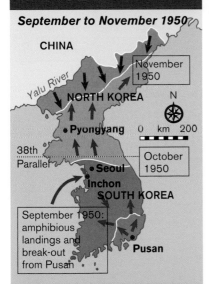

On 1 October they crossed the 38th Parallel and pushed on towards the border with China. As they did so, the Chinese leader, Mao Zedong, warned the UN forces to withdraw.

Stage 3

In November 1950 200,000 Chinese 'volunteers' armed by the USSR invaded North Korea, crossing the Yalu River. The UN forces were driven back to the 38th Parallel. The war became a stalemate where the armies had halted.

In March 1951 MacArthur proposed attacking China directly. Truman still stuck to his policy of containment, but the UN Commander seemed to be suggesting expansion and conquest. The dangers of nuclear war, particularly since China had Soviet backing, were clear. MacArthur was sacked.

In June 1951 peace talks began, but the fighting around the 38th Parallel continued until July 1953. New peace talks once again divided North and South Korea along the 38th Parallel.

The Korean War brought the superpowers close to direct conflict. This intensified with the arms race and the development of alliances across the world.

Khrushchev and peaceful coexistence

🔑 Key points, 1955–63

- Khrushchev
- Hungary
- Space and the arms race
- U2 spy-plane
- Berlin Wall
- Kennedy v Khrushchev

The end of the Stalinist era

Stalin died in 1953. By 1955 Nikita Khrushchev was leader of the USSR. He was a reformer. He wanted a change in foreign policy, and a move away from heavy industry and rearmament towards producing more food and consumer goods.

Peaceful coexistence?

In February 1956 Khrushchev used the Twentieth Party Congress of the Soviet Communist Party to attack Stalin for tyranny, cruelty and self-glorification. Khrushchev seemed to be proposing a period of de-Stalinisation. He wanted the Communist and capitalist worlds to live side-by-side in 'peaceful coexistence'. The authoritarianism of the Communist Party was being questioned and undermined.

The people of Eastern Europe disliked the Soviet 'Big Brother'. But would Khrushchev allow the strict control by the USSR of Eastern Europe to relax?

Landmarks
1953: Death of Stalin leads to thaw in East–West relations
1955: Warsaw Pact signed as a military alliance of the Iron Curtain countries
1956: Khrushchev denounces Stalin — leads to uprisings in Poland and Hungary

1961: East Germany builds the Berlin Wall to stop refugees leaving East Germany for West Germany

1956: Riots put down with the help of Russians. New government led by Gomulka gives Poles more freedom

1953: Workers go on strike. Fears in Russia of an uprising. Soviet tanks put down the unrest

Uprising in Hungary in 1956. New leader Imre Nagy introduces liberal reforms and Khrushchev fears Hungary may leave the Communist bloc. Soviet tanks put down the rebellion with loss of over 20,000 lives. Nagy is executed and replaced by Kádár

Marshal Tito establishes his own brand of Communism

Breaks with Russia in 1961

Russia's most reliable ally in Eastern Europe

Unrest in Eastern Europe after Stalin's death

The evidence indicates otherwise.

◆ In East Berlin (1953) a General Strike was crushed by Soviet tanks.

◆ In Poland (1956) there were riots and demonstrations, mainly about food prices. Soviet tanks went to Warsaw to restore order, although a more popular Communist leader, Wladyslaw Gomulka, was allowed to take charge.

◆ The Hungarians hated the strict Communist control from their leader, Rakosi. He took his orders from Moscow. Hungarians also had a weak economy and there was anger about poverty, low living standards and food shortages. There was no freedom of speech and no free elections. The secret police held thousands of political prisoners in jail.

The Hungarian Rising, 1956

Rakosi was forced to resign. Under another more popular leader, Nagy, Hungary took a dangerous path. He wanted free elections, so that people from outside the Communist Party could be voted into the government. But for Moscow, the last straw was when Hungary wanted to leave the Warsaw Pact and become neutral. The Russians complained that things seemed to be out of control there, because of violent demonstrations which were taking place. Thousands of Soviet tanks rolled into Hungary and the rising was crushed. 30,000 Hungarians lost their lives. Kadar became the new leader, with Moscow's approval.

Summit conferences

In 1958 another crisis seemed to be developing over Berlin. Thousands of East Berliners were escaping to West Germany via West Berlin. Khrushchev talked of isolating the city again. However, in 1959 he went to meet President Eisenhower at Camp David in the USA. Was this a hopeful sign? They agreed to meet again the following year in Paris. But the spirit of negotiation soon ended.

The U2 incident, 1960

Shortly before the Paris Summit, an American U2 spy–plane was shot down over the USSR. The pilot, Gary Powers, was taken prisoner. Khrushchev accused the Americans of deceit and asked for an apology and a promise that there would be no more spy flights. There was no apology and the conference collapsed before it had begun.

The Berlin Wall, 1961

'Peaceful coexistence' was again put to the test in 1961. Thousands of refugees were fleeing from the East, crossing to West Berlin where there was the prospect of a better standard of living and attractive consumer goods in the shops. Khrushchev ordered the building of a wall, protected by barbed wire, to stop the East Berliners escaping. It divided the city and made relations between Khrushchev and the new US President, John F. Kennedy, very difficult. Kennedy promised 'to defend liberty wherever it is threatened' but took no other action, even though American and Russian tanks faced each other across the Wall. Khrushchev would test the new President's nerve again, in 1962.

Exam watch

How did the Cold War become a global conflict, 1950–61? How successfully did the USA contain Communism during this period? How far was 'peaceful coexistence' a complete failure up to 1961?

War over Cuba?

The Arms Race and the Space Race

The USA and USSR began a hugely expensive 'race' to gain the upper hand in weapons and space technology.

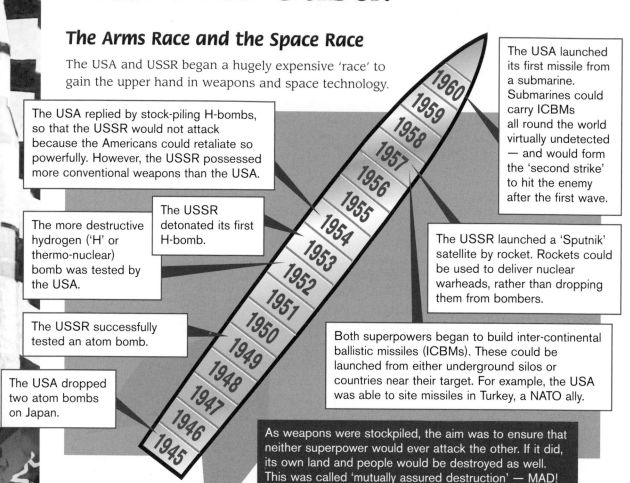

The USA launched its first missile from a submarine. Submarines could carry ICBMs all round the world virtually undetected — and would form the 'second strike' to hit the enemy after the first wave.

The USA replied by stock-piling H-bombs, so that the USSR would not attack because the Americans could retaliate so powerfully. However, the USSR possessed more conventional weapons than the USA.

The USSR detonated its first H-bomb.

The more destructive hydrogen ('H' or thermo-nuclear) bomb was tested by the USA.

The USSR launched a 'Sputnik' satellite by rocket. Rockets could be used to deliver nuclear warheads, rather than dropping them from bombers.

The USSR successfully tested an atom bomb.

Both superpowers began to build inter-continental ballistic missiles (ICBMs). These could be launched from either underground silos or countries near their target. For example, the USA was able to site missiles in Turkey, a NATO ally.

The USA dropped two atom bombs on Japan.

As weapons were stockpiled, the aim was to ensure that neither superpower would ever attack the other. If it did, its own land and people would be destroyed as well. This was called 'mutually assured destruction' — MAD!

1960
1959
1958
1957
1956
1955
1954
1953
1952
1951
1950
1949
1948
1947
1946
1945

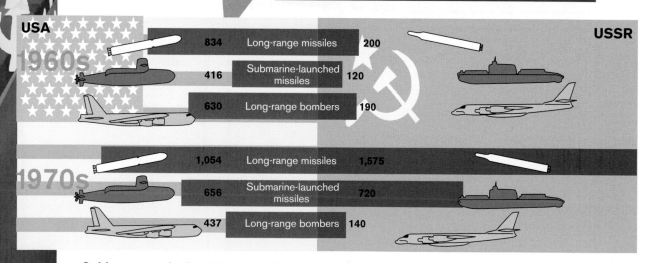

USA   **USSR**

1960s

	USA		USSR
Long-range missiles	834		200
Submarine-launched missiles	416		120
Long-range bombers	630		190

1970s

	USA		USSR
Long-range missiles	1,054		1,575
Submarine-launched missiles	656		720
Long-range bombers	437		140

Cold war arms in the 1960s and 1970s

The Cuban Missile Crisis, 1962

Cuba is very close to the USA. In the 1950s American businesses owned property in Cuba and had invested heavily in the island.

In 1959 the Cuban government of President Batista was overthrown by a Communist, Fidel Castro. Relations between the USA and Cuba quickly worsened.

Map labels:
- US missile launching base
- BLOCKADE ZONE
- Cape Canaveral
- 25 Russian merchant ships approaching Cuba. Some are carrying planes and missiles
- US air and naval bases in Florida
- Homestead
- Key West
- Havana
- CUBA
- US air and naval base on Cuba
- Soviet missile sites
- Guantánamo
- HAITI
- JAMAICA
- N
- 0 km 400
- 180 warships in Task Force 136 enforce the American blockade

Stages in the crisis

1 In 1960 Castro took over land and businesses owned by Americans.

2 The USA banned trade with Cuba, in an effort to cripple Castro. The USSR stepped in to help, by buying Cuba's vital sugar crop.

3 The US army secretly trained men loyal to Batista in guerrilla warfare.

4 In April 1961 President Kennedy helped 1,600 Cuban exiles to invade Cuba at the Bay of Pigs. The Communists easily rounded up Batista's men, which embarrassed Kennedy and further cemented relations between Moscow and Cuba.

5 Khrushchev decided that Cuba could be used as a site for Soviet missiles. They would be able to reach all parts of the USA, except the north-western cities. To Khrushchev, this was a reply to American missiles stationed in Turkey.

6 In October 1962, US spy-planes photographed Soviet missile sites on Cuba. What would Kennedy do?

7 On 22 October Kennedy announced that there would be a naval blockade of Cuba. Ships in the quarantine zone would be searched and any carrying missiles would be sent back.

8 In the following days a fleet of Soviet merchant ships was detected approaching Cuba. US troops were sent to Florida. The risk of armed conflict was palpable: the world feared global destruction. Behind the scenes, talks took place between the two sides.

9 On 28 October Khrushchev agreed to remove Soviet missiles and missile sites from Cuba, on condition that there would be no US invasion of the island.

10 On 2 November the blockade was lifted.

Results

- The world had gone to the brink of war. Kennedy and Khrushchev recognised the importance of reducing tension and took steps to support peace.
- In 1963 a telephone 'hotline' was set up between the White House and the Kremlin.
- Nuclear arms talks began. In 1963 a Nuclear Test Ban Treaty was signed.

 Exam watch

How close to war did the world come over Cuba in 1962? What were the results of the Cuban Crisis?

The Vietnam War

Setting the scene

- Before the Second World War, Vietnam was ruled by France. During the war, Japan overran Vietnam and exploited it for its rice, coal and rubber.
- In 1941 the Vietminh was formed by Ho Chi Minh as a resistance movement. Supported by American weapons and supplies, it led an uprising against the Japanese in 1945.

- After 1946, France tried to reassert control over the south of Vietnam and took over the northern city of Haiphong.
- The Vietminh took control of the countryside, fighting a guerrilla war against the French who controlled the cities. Ho Chi Minh was supported by China and the USSR.
- Despite US help, to France the human cost was crippling — 74,000 dead French soldiers by 1953 — as well as the financial cost.
- The Vietminh avoided open battle. The French attempted to lure them out into the open by fortifying the garrison at Dien Bien Phu. The Vietminh managed to supply 40,000 guerrillas, surrounding the French base and cutting it off. The French were defeated and humiliated.

Peace talks at Geneva (1954) agreed that:
- Vietnam was to be divided into North and South, along the 17th Parallel.
- Laos and Cambodia were to become independent states.
- The French would withdraw.
- Elections would take place in 2 years to reunite the country.

US involvement

The elections never took place. General Ngo Dinh Diem established an unpopular dictatorship in the South and, with US economic and military advisers, began a campaign to root out the Vietminh. By the early 1960s it had become the aim of North Vietnam to 'liberate' the South and unite the country.

Guerrilla attacks by Communist fighters (the Vietcong) intensified and Diem became even more unpopular. He moved peasants away from the land their families had farmed for years to 'fortified villages'. He also persecuted Buddhists; one monk, Quang Duc, protested by setting himself on fire. Meanwhile, US forces became increasingly committed to the defence of the South.

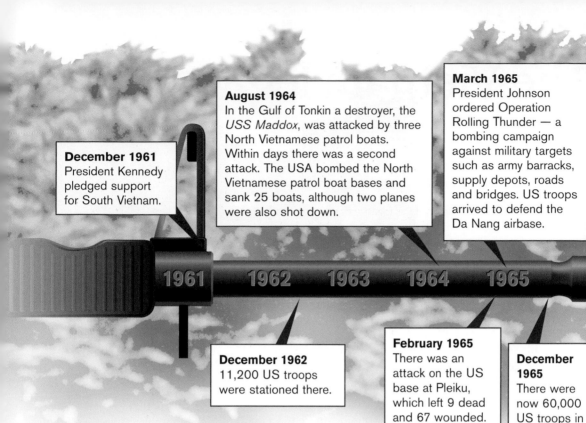

December 1961
President Kennedy pledged support for South Vietnam.

August 1964
In the Gulf of Tonkin a destroyer, the *USS Maddox*, was attacked by three North Vietnamese patrol boats. Within days there was a second attack. The USA bombed the North Vietnamese patrol boat bases and sank 25 boats, although two planes were also shot down.

March 1965
President Johnson ordered Operation Rolling Thunder — a bombing campaign against military targets such as army barracks, supply depots, roads and bridges. US troops arrived to defend the Da Nang airbase.

1961   1962   1963   1964   1965

December 1962
11,200 US troops were stationed there.

February 1965
There was an attack on the US base at Pleiku, which left 9 dead and 67 wounded.

December 1965
There were now 60,000 US troops in Vietnam.

Guerrilla tactics

Why did the US find it so difficult to defeat the Vietcong? Guerrilla strategy was based on avoiding open combat, since the Vietcong had inferior numbers and weapons against a technologically superior enemy. Vietcong tactics proved highly effective. They were to:

◆ gain the support of the villages
◆ attack in small groups by ambush and then disappear into the jungle
◆ spread revolutionary ideas among the peasants
◆ use networks of booby-trapped tunnels as underground shelters and supply dumps
◆ use secret routes through the jungle (like the Ho Chi Minh Trail) to keep the troops supplied
◆ target and murder local officials

In reply, the US forces found it difficult to identify the Vietcong; they would just 'melt away' into their village communities. US tactics became increasingly desperate.

◆ Saturation or 'blanket' bombing from B52s was introduced. More bombs were dropped on Vietnam than were used to bomb Europe during the whole of the Second World War.
◆ Search and destroy missions were undertaken, using helicopters to target particular villages. Whole villages were destroyed in attempts to identify Vietcong guerrillas.
◆ Chemical defoliants such as 'Agent Orange' were used to clear millions of acres of jungle, depriving the Vietcong of cover.

 Exam watch

Why did the United States become involved in Vietnam? Why was it difficult for the US to win the war?

The Vietnam legacy

The protest movement

There was growing opposition to the war inside the USA:

Anti-war demonstrators at Kent State University, May 1970

- Young men opposed the draft (conscription).
- Anti-war demonstrations intensified as the death rate of US soldiers increased. In November 1968, 38,000 people demonstrated outside the White House. War veterans and students joined forces in angry protests. When 10,000 demonstrated outside the Democratic Convention in Chicago in 1968, there were violent clashes with the police.
- In May 1970, a peaceful protest by around 2,000 students at Kent State University in Ohio ended in bloodshed when National Guardsmen opened fire, killing four students and wounding another nine.

Demands for peace

Americans were divided about whether the USA should 'bring the boys home'. Opposition to the war grew in 1968 because of:

Media coverage
Television pictures from the war took powerful images into the homes of Americans. As the 'body count' grew, people became disillusioned. They questioned whether this was really a war to defend freedom and democracy against Communist tyranny. They could see for themselves the effects of blanket bombing and the use of chemicals and napalm on civilians and villages.

Americans also began to think that the war could not be won.

The Tet Offensive
In a coordinated onslaught, the North Vietnamese army and Vietcong were able to attack 100 cities throughout the South, including Saigon, where fighting was intense. The US Embassy in Saigon was taken over for 6 hours; America was stunned.

Although the US and South Vietnamese forces defeated the Communist offensive and weakened the Vietcong, the American public was surprised by its scale. Demands for withdrawal grew.

The My Lai massacre
When US soldiers on a 'search and destroy' mission massacred over 300 villagers and burnt their homes, the atrocity caught the public's attention. Revulsion at the indiscriminate killing fuelled opposition in America to the war.

The escalating cost
Under President Johnson (1964–68) the US faced inflation and rising welfare costs. His aim to create a 'great society' was being undermined by what he called 'a bitch of a war'.

When President Nixon was elected in 1968, peace talks in Paris were opened, as he had promised. In the meantime, the war continued. By 1969, costs had soared to $30 billion.

The role of individuals

Throughout the peace talks **President Nixon** kept up pressure on the North, with sustained bombing raids on Hanoi and the Ho Chi Minh Trail between 1970 and 1972.

He visited China and the USSR to improve relations with the Communist world. His policy of 'Vietnamisation' committed Nixon to withdrawing US troops and training and supplying the ARVN (South Vietnam's army). Behind the scenes, secret talks took place in 1972 between **Henry Kissinger** (the US Secretary of State) and **Le Duc Tho** of North Vietnam. Progress was slow, so Nixon again applied pressure with 11 days of massive bombing raids on Hanoi and Haiphong.

The North restarted talks and a ceasefire was arranged for January 1973. In March the last US combat troops left Vietnam. American aid to South Vietnam fell significantly.

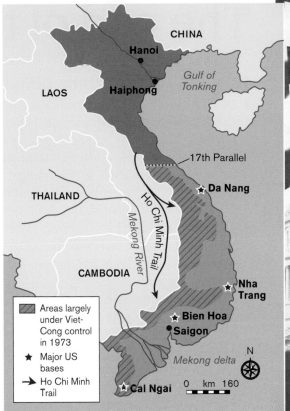

The final battles

Ho Chi Minh had not given up the fight for the South. In 1974 the war restarted. Da Nang fell to the Communists in March 1975. Saigon was captured in April. Vietnam became a single country under a Communist government.

Results of the war

1 America's role as world policeman had been undermined. Communism scored a victory against the policy of containment. America's moral stature was tarnished by its military tactics. Vietnam veterans felt that America had turned its back on them when they returned home.

2 Vietnam suffered greatly from the effects of the war. Environmental damage (from the use of chemicals) meant poorer crops and starvation, which held the country back for many years.

3 Communist rule led to the collectivisation of agriculture and nationalised industries. Skilled professionals fled Vietnam, as well as over a million 'boat people'. Trade sanctions and further wars against Cambodia and China added to its economic problems. Recovery did not begin until 1993, when the IMF and World Bank provided loans.

Exam watch

Focus on why the United States became involved in Vietnam, and then found it so difficult to defeat the Communists.

What were the most important reasons for US withdrawal? What role did the media play in the peace movement? What have been the short- and long-term effects of the war on the USA and on Vietnam?

The end of the Cold War

Why did détente come about?

- Despite the introduction of the 'hot line', the Cuban Missile Crisis exposed the 'balance of terror' caused by the existence of so many weapons of mass destruction. Added to this were fears that nuclear weapons might 'proliferate' and be developed by a number of smaller countries.

> **détente:** a relaxing of tension between the superpowers, brought about through summit meetings between the leaders of the USA and USSR, thereby attempting to limit the growth of nuclear weapons

- The world remained a dangerous place because of the quarrel which had broken out between the USSR and Communist China. Each side denounced the other for betraying Communism; relations deteriorated further because of border disputes between the two Communist giants.
- China wanted to increase trade with the West.
- The USSR faced dissent on its borders. It wished to focus on these problems. For example, in 1968 Alexander Dubček became leader of Czechoslovakia. He wanted 'socialism with a human face', with less repression and more freedom. The Soviet leader, Brezhnev, regarded these signs of independence as dangerous, so tanks were sent in to crush the rebellion.
- The cost of the arms race was proving crippling to all sides.

The rise and fall of détente

Tension decreased

1 In 1969 Strategic Arms Limitation talks (SALT) began between the USSR and USA.

2 In 1971 Communist China joined the United Nations.

3 In 1972 President Nixon visited China.

4 Also in 1972 the 'SALT 1' treaty was signed between the USA and USSR, restricting anti-ballistic missile defence systems.

5 In 1975 the Helsinki Agreement was signed, laying down an international basis for the recognition of human rights while Brezhnev (USSR) and Carter (USA) accepted European borders as they stood.

Then tension increased again

6 In 1979 the USSR invaded Afghanistan. The USA protested and refused to sign 'SALT 2' — a new agreement limiting nuclear missiles.

7 In 1981 Ronald Reagan became President of the USA. He took a harder line with the USSR, referring to it as the 'evil empire'.

8 In 1983 'Star Wars' was announced — the USA would develop weapons in space to destroy incoming missiles. Was this a new arms race?

9 Also in 1983 cruise missiles (new ground-launched weapons) were sent to bases in Europe. Strategic Arms Reduction Treaty (START) talks collapsed, because of Soviet anger over the arrival of cruise missiles on its doorstep.

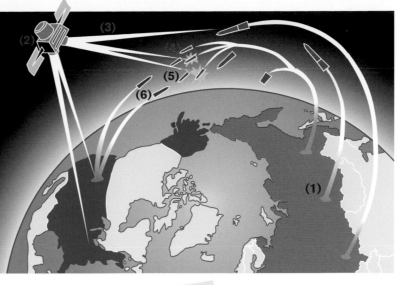

As soon as Soviet ICBMs are launched (1), American 'killer satellites' (2) use laser-beam weapons (3), to destroy them or their warheads (4). Any warheads that escape (5) are taken out by ground-based ABMs (anti-ballistic missiles) (6). To be effective the system has to be 'leak-proof', with no warheads getting through, but high cost and futuristic technology raised doubts about Star Wars becoming a reality.

The Star Wars concept

Gorbachev and the end of the Cold War

Mikhail Gorbachev was the leader of the Soviet Union, 1985–91. He wanted changes in Soviet policies at home and abroad because of events both inside and outside the Soviet Union (see page 74).

Russians had a low standard of living, rising prices and falling wages. Serious crime and corruption were on the increase, while the state kept strict controls over the press and denied people freedom of expression and action. The cost of the arms race drained the USSR of resources. It was pursuing an unpopular war in Afghanistan and remained the focus of East Europeans' anger.

The collapse of the Communist world happened with bewildering speed. Throughout 1989, the Iron Curtain was being undermined. Free elections in Poland brought a reformer, Lech Wałęsa, to power. In the USSR Gorbachev encouraged more discussion of government policies in a Peoples' Congress.

Demonstrations against the government in East Germany gathered pace and, in November, the Berlin Wall was torn down by demonstrators. There could be no more powerful symbol of the end of the Cold War than that. Romania's Communist leader was killed. In 1989 and 1990 free elections took place in Bulgaria, Hungary and Czechoslovakia. The Communists were in retreat. Even in Russia, non-Communist parties were formed and competed for power. Germany was reunited and became a member of NATO. Eastern Europe no longer confronted the West — it wanted to join it.

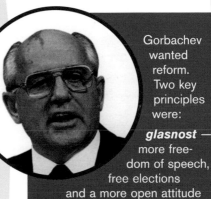

Gorbachev wanted reform. Two key principles were:

glasnost — more freedom of speech, free elections and a more open attitude throughout government

perestroika — less state control of the economy and freer markets, so that people could buy and sell as they wished, giving them a greater incentive to work hard

 Exam watch

How far was détente a success? How and why did détente collapse in the late 1970s and early 1980s? Why did Communism collapse so quickly?